بسم الله الرحمن الرحيم

# *The Art of Learning*

TIMELESS WISDOM FOR THE SEEKER OF KNOWLEDGE

**THE ART OF LEARNING**
**A TRANSLATION OF** *Taʿlīm al-Mutaʿallim Ṭarīq al-Taʿallum*



**IMAM GHAZALI PUBLISHING**
NEW YORK, USA
INFO@IMAMGHAZALI.CO
**WWW.IMAMGHAZALI.CO**

**BULK ORDERING INFORMATION:** SPECIAL DISCOUNTS ARE AVAILABLE ON QUANTITY PURCHASES. FOR DETAILS, PLEASE CONTACT THE DISTRIBUTORS:

**SATTAUR PUBLISHING**
INFO@SATTAURPUBLISHING.COM
**WWW.SATTAURPUBLISHING.COM**

PRINTED IN THE USA, UK, MALAYSIA, AND INDIA



ISBN: 978-1-966329-00-8

FIRST EDITION

10 9 8 7 6 5 4 3 2 1

# *The Art of Learning*

TIMELESS WISDOM FOR THE SEEKER OF KNOWLEDGE

A NEW TRANSLATION OF

*Taʿlīm al-Mutaʿallim Ṭarīq al-Taʿallum*

Burhān al-Dīn al-Zarnūjī

*Translated by Shams Tameez*

# CONTENTS

# AL-ZARNŪJĪ & HIS WORK

Burhān al-Dīn al-Zarnūjī was a leading scholar and educational theorist from the 6th century AH (12th century CE). He is best known for his seminal work *Taʿlīm al-Mutaʿallim Ṭarīq al-Taʿallum* (the work you now hold in your hands), a widely respected pedagogical work with focus on the ethics and methods of seeking knowledge in the Islamic tradition.

Al-Zarnūjī was born in the town of Zarnūj, located beyond the Oxus River (Āmū Daryā) in the modern Turkistan region of Kazakhstan. His full name is commonly believed to be Nuʿmān ibn Ibrāhīm, though historical records vary slightly on this detail. His agnomen, *Burhān al-Dīn* (Proof of the Faith) and *Burhān al-Islām* (Proof of Islam), reflects his significant contributions to Islamic scholarship and the moral dimensions of education.

He received his early education in Zarnūj before studying under several influential scholars of his time. Among his teachers were Shaykh Burhān al-Dīn ʿAlī ibn Abī Bakr al-Marghīnānī, the author of *Al-Hidāyah*, a foundational text in Ḥanafī jurisprudence; Shaykh Abū al-Muḥāmid Qawādud-dīn Ḥammād ibn Ibrāhīm al-Ṣaffār; and Shaykh Ḥasan ibn Manṣūr Qāḍiykhānī. These teachers were part of the rich intellectual environment of Central Asia, where jurisprudence, ethics, and spirituality were taught with a focus on personal development and societal contribution.

The historical records do not provide a precise date of his death, but it is generally estimated that he passed away around 620 AH (1223 CE) in Bukhārā, a prominent intellectual hub in the medieval Islamic world.

Though little is known about his life, Al-Zarnūjī's legacy rests primarily on his treatise *Taʿlīm al-Mutaʿallim Ṭarīq al-Taʿallum*, which offers a detailed ethical and methodological guide for students and teachers alike. The work is divided into several chapters, covering key aspects of the educational process. These include the merits and purpose of knowledge, the importance of intention, selecting a teacher and companions, respect for knowledge, perseverance, and the spiritual dimensions of learning such as sincerity, humility, and trust in Allah (*tawakkul*). Al-Zarnūjī believed that true learning requires both intellectual effort and spiritual refinement, making his work foundational in Islamic pedagogy.

His influence extends far beyond his lifetime. *Taʿlīm al-Mutaʿallim* became a standard text in Islamic seminaries and traditional educational institutions, especially in regions like the former Ottoman domain, Central Asia, the Indian subcontinent and Southeast Asia. It continues to be a key component of the curriculum in many Islamic seminaries.

The work's widespread popularity led to the production of numerous commentaries and translations over the centuries. Its first known translations appeared in the 19$^{th}$ century.

# *The Art of Learning*

## IN THE NAME OF ALLAH, THE MOST GRACIOUS, THE MOST MERCIFUL

All praise is due to Allah, who has elevated the children of Adam through knowledge and action above all creation. Blessings and peace be upon Muhammad, the leader of both Arabs and non-Arabs, and upon his family and companions, the fountains of knowledge and wisdom.

*To proceed:*

When I observed that many students of knowledge in our time strive earnestly in their pursuit yet fail to attain it, and remain deprived of its benefits and fruits – namely, practising it and spreading it – I realised this was because they had erred in their approach and neglected its conditions. Whoever errs in the path goes astray and will not achieve the intended goal, whether minor or major.

Therefore, I desired and resolved to clarify for them the correct way to seek knowledge based on what I have read in books and heard from my esteemed teachers, the possessors of knowledge and wisdom. This effort is made with the hope that those who are sincere and eager for this guidance will pray for my success and salvation on the Day of Judgment. After seeking Allah's guidance in this endeavour, I have titled it: *Instruction for the Student: The Path to Learning.*

I have divided it into the following:

- A chapter on the essence of knowledge, jurisprudence, and its virtues.
- A chapter on the intention during learning.
- A chapter on choosing the field of study, the teacher, the companion, and persistence.
- A chapter on honouring knowledge and its people.
- A chapter on diligence, consistency, and aspiration.
- A chapter on the beginning of study, its extent, and its

بِسْمِ اللهِ الرَّحْمٰنِ الرَّحِيمِ

الْحَمْدُ لِلَّهِ الَّذِي فَضَّلَ بَنِي آدَمَ بِالْعِلْمِ وَالْعَمَلِ عَلَى جَمِيعِ الْعَالَمِ، وَالصَّلَاةُ وَالسَّلَامُ عَلَى مُحَمَّدٍ سَيِّدِ الْعَرَبِ وَالْعَجَمِ، وَعَلَى آلِهِ وَأَصْحَابِهِ يَنَابِيعِ الْعُلُومِ وَالْحِكَمِ.

وَبَعْدُ:

فَلَمَّا رَأَيْتُ كَثِيرًا مِنْ طُلَّابِ الْعِلْمِ فِي زَمَانِنَا يَجِدُّونَ إِلَى الْعِلْمِ وَلَا يَصِلُونَ، وَمِنْ مَنَافِعِهِ وَثَمَرَاتِهِ - وَهِيَ الْعَمَلُ بِهِ وَالنَّشْرُ - يُحْرَمُونَ؛ لِمَا أَنَّهُمْ أَخْطَأُوا طَرِيقَهُ وَتَرَكُوا شَرَائِطَهُ، وَكُلُّ مَنْ أَخْطَأَ الطَّرِيقَ ضَلَّ، وَلَا يَنَالُ الْمَقْصُودَ قَلَّ أَوْ جَلَّ، فَأَرَدْتُ وَأَحْبَبْتُ أَنْ أُبَيِّنَ لَهُمْ طَرِيقَ التَّعَلُّمِ عَلَى مَا رَأَيْتُ فِي الْكُتُبِ، وَسَمِعْتُ مِنْ أَسَاتِيذِي أُولِي الْعِلْمِ وَالْحِكَمِ رَجَاءَ الدُّعَاءِ لِي مِنَ الرَّاغِبِينَ فِيهِ، الْمُخْلَصِينَ، بِالْفَوْزِ وَالْخَلَاصِ فِي يَوْمِ الدِّينِ، بَعْدَمَا اسْتَخَرْتُ اللَّهَ تَعَالَى فِيهِ، وَسَمَّيْتُهُ: «تَعْلِيمَ الْمُتَعَلِّمِ طَرِيقَ التَّعَلُّمِ».

وَجَعَلْتُهُ فُصُولًا:

فَصْلٌ: فِي مَاهِيَّةِ الْعِلْمِ، وَالْفِقْهِ، وَفَضْلِهِ.

فَصْلٌ: فِي النِّيَّةِ فِي حَالِ التَّعَلُّمِ.

فَصْلٌ: فِي اخْتِيَارِ الْعِلْمِ، وَالْأُسْتَاذِ، وَالشَّرِيكِ، وَالثَّبَاتِ.

فَصْلٌ: فِي تَعْظِيمِ الْعِلْمِ وَأَهْلِهِ.

فَصْلٌ: فِي الْجِدِّ وَالْمُوَاظَبَةِ وَالْهِمَّةِ.

organisation.

- A chapter on reliance upon Allah.
- A chapter on the appropriate times for acquiring knowledge.
- A chapter on compassion and giving sincere advice.
- A chapter on benefiting from learning and acquiring proper conduct.
- A chapter on mindfulness during learning.
- A chapter on what aids memory and what causes forgetfulness.
- A chapter on what brings sustenance and what prevents it, and what increases one's lifespan and what diminishes it.

My success lies only with Allah; upon Him I rely, and to Him I turn in repentance.

فَصْلٌ: فِي بِدَايَةِ السَّبْقِ وَقَدْرِهِ وَتَرْتِيبِهِ.
فَصْلٌ: فِي التَّوَكُّلِ.
فَصْلٌ: فِي وَقْتِ التَّحْصِيلِ.
فَصْلٌ: فِي الشَّفَقَةِ وَالنَّصِيحَةِ.
فَصْلٌ: فِي الاِسْتِفَادَةِ وَاقْتِبَاسِ الْأَدَبِ.
فَصْلٌ: فِي الْوَرَعِ فِي حَالَةِ التَّعَلُّمِ.
فَصْلٌ: فِيمَا يُوَرِّثُ الْحِفْظَ، وَفِيمَا يُوَرِّثُ النِّسْيَانَ.
فَصْلٌ: فِيمَا يَجْلِبُ الرِّزْقَ، وَفِيمَا يَمْنَعُ، وَمَا يَزِيدُ فِي الْعُمْرِ، وَمَا يُنْقِصُ.
وَمَا تَوْفِيقِي إِلَّا بِاللَّهِ عَلَيْهِ تَوَكَّلْتُ وَإِلَيْهِ أُنِيبُ.

## THE NATURE OF KNOWLEDGE, JURISPRUDENCE, AND ITS VIRTUES

The Messenger of Allah ﷺ said: "Seeking knowledge is an obligation upon every Muslim, male and female." Know that it is not obligatory for every Muslim to seek all forms of knowledge. Rather, the obligation pertains to acquiring the knowledge relevant to one's current circumstances, as it is said: "The best knowledge is the knowledge of one's present state, and the best action is safeguarding that state."

It is incumbent upon a Muslim to seek knowledge pertaining to his situation, whatever it may be. For example, since prayer is obligatory, it is mandatory to learn the necessary knowledge of prayer to fulfil its obligations correctly. Similarly, one must acquire sufficient knowledge to perform obligatory duties, for whatever leads to the fulfilment of an obligation becomes itself obligatory. Likewise, what facilitates the fulfilment of a mandatory act becomes mandatory.

The same principle applies to fasting, *zakāh* (if one possesses wealth), and Hajj (if it becomes obligatory). Similarly, in trade and business transactions, one must learn the rules that prevent engaging in prohibited practices.

It is reported that someone once asked Muhammad ibn al-Ḥasan ؒ: "Why don't you write a book on asceticism (*zuhd*)?" He replied: "I have written a book on trade." By this, he implied that true asceticism involves avoiding doubtful and disliked practices in one's transactions.

The same applies to all other dealings and professions. Anyone engaged in such activities must acquire knowledge to avoid what is prohibited. Furthermore, it is obligatory to understand the states of the heart, such as reliance on Allah, turning to Him in repentance, fear of Him, and contentment, as these qualities are relevant to all circumstances.

The nobility of knowledge is evident to all; it is uniquely

## فَصْلٌ فِي مَاهِيَّةِ الْعِلْمِ، وَالْفِقْهِ، وَفَضْلِهِ

قَالَ رَسُولُ اللَّهِ ﷺ : «طَلَبُ الْعِلْمِ فَرِيضَةٌ عَلَىٰ كُلِّ مُسْلِمٍ وَمُسْلِمَةٍ».
اعْلَمْ بِأَنَّهُ لَا يُفْتَرَضُ عَلَىٰ كُلِّ مُسْلِمٍ طَلَبُ كُلِّ عِلْمٍ، وَإِنَّمَا يُفْتَرَضُ عَلَيْهِ طَلَبُ عِلْمِ الْحَالِ، كَمَا يُقَالُ: «وَأَفْضَلُ الْعِلْمِ عِلْمُ الْحَالِ، وَأَفْضَلُ الْعَمَلِ حِفْظُ الْحَالِ».

وَيُفْتَرَضُ عَلَى الْمُسْلِمِ طَلَبُ مَا يَقَعُ لَهُ فِي حَالِهِ، فِي أَيِّ حَالٍ كَانَ، فَإِنَّهُ لَا بُدَّ لَهُ مِنَ الصَّلَاةِ، فَيُفْتَرَضُ عَلَيْهِ عِلْمُ مَا يَقَعُ لَهُ فِي صَلَاتِهِ بِقَدْرِ مَا يُؤَدِّي بِهِ فَرْضَ الصَّلَاةِ، وَيَجِبُ عَلَيْهِ بِقَدْرِ مَا يُؤَدِّي بِهِ الْوَاجِبَ؛ لِأَنَّ مَا يُتَوَسَّلُ بِهِ إِلَىٰ إِقَامَةِ الْفَرْضِ يَكُونُ فَرْضًا، وَمَا يُتَوَسَّلُ بِهِ إِلَىٰ إِقَامَةِ الْوَاجِبِ يَكُونُ وَاجِبًا.

وَكَذَلِكَ فِي الصَّوْمِ، وَالزَّكَاةِ إِنْ كَانَ لَهُ مَالٌ، وَالْحَجِّ إِنْ وَجَبَ عَلَيْهِ، وَكَذَلِكَ فِي الْبُيُوعِ إِنْ كَانَ يَتَّجِرُ.

قِيلَ : لِمُحَمَّدِ بْنِ الْحَسَنِ رَحْمَةُ اللَّهِ عَلَيْهِ : لِمَ لَا تُصَنِّفُ كِتَابًا فِي الزُّهْدِ؟ قَالَ: قَدْ صَنَّفْتُ كِتَابًا فِي الْبُيُوعِ. يَعْنِي الزَّاهِدُ مَنْ يَحْتَرِزُ عَنِ الشُّبُهَاتِ وَالْمَكْرُوهَاتِ فِي التِّجَارَاتِ.

وَكَذَلِكَ فِي سَائِرِ الْمُعَامَلَاتِ وَالْحِرَفِ، وَكُلُّ مَنِ اشْتَغَلَ بِشَيْءٍ مِنْهَا يُفْتَرَضُ عَلَيْهِ عِلْمُ التَّحَرُّزِ عَنِ الْحَرَامِ فِيهِ، وَكَذَلِكَ يُفْتَرَضُ عَلَيْهِ عِلْمُ أَحْوَالِ الْقَلْبِ مِنَ التَّوَكُّلِ وَالْإِنَابَةِ وَالْخَشْيَةِ وَالرِّضَى؛ فَإِنَّهُ وَاقِعٌ فِي جَمِيعِ الْأَحْوَالِ.

associated with humanity. All other virtues, except knowledge, are shared between humans and other creatures, such as courage, boldness, strength, generosity, and compassion, among others.

Through knowledge, Allah Almighty demonstrated the superiority of Adam ﷺ over the angels, commanding them to prostrate to him. Knowledge is esteemed because it serves as a means to righteousness and piety, which enables a person to attain honour with Allah and eternal happiness. As was advised to Muhammad ibn al-Ḥasan ﷺ:

*Seek knowledge, for knowledge is an adornment for its people,*
*A virtue, and the foundation for all commendable qualities.*
*Strive each day to increase your knowledge,*
*And immerse yourself in the seas of benefits.*
*Understand jurisprudence, for it is the best guide*
*To righteousness and piety, the most just aim.*
*It is the guiding light leading to the paths of guidance;*
*It is the fortress that saves from all calamities.*
*Indeed, a single pious jurist is more formidable*
*Against Satan than a thousand worshippers.*

Knowledge is a means to understand qualities such as arrogance, humility, camaraderie, modesty, extravagance, and miserliness, among others. It also pertains to all other moral traits, including generosity, stinginess, cowardice, and boldness.

Arrogance, miserliness, cowardice, and extravagance are forbidden, and one cannot avoid them except through knowledge of these vices and what opposes them. Thus, it is obligatory for every individual to acquire knowledge of these matters.

The Sayyid, the esteemed imam, martyr, and teacher, Nāsir al-Dīn Abū al-Qāsim has compiled a book on ethics (*akhlāq*), which is indeed a commendable work. It is obligatory for every Muslim to memorise its contents.

As for the knowledge that pertains to one's own circum-

وَشَرَفُ الْعِلْمِ لَا يَخْفَىٰ عَلَىٰ أَحَدٍ؛ إِذْ هُوَ الْمُخْتَصُّ بِالْإِنْسَانِيَّةِ؛ لِأَنَّ جَمِيعَ الْخِصَالِ سِوَى الْعِلْمِ يَشْتَرِكُ فِيهَا الْإِنْسَانُ وَسَائِرُ الْحَيَوَانَاتِ؛ كَالشَّجَاعَةِ، وَالْجَرَاءَةِ، وَالْقُوَّةِ، وَالْجُودِ، وَالشَّفَقَةِ وَغَيْرِهَا سِوَى الْعِلْمِ. وَبِهِ أَظْهَرَ اللَّهُ تَعَالَىٰ فَضْلَ آدَمَ عَلَيْهِ السَّلَامُ عَلَى الْمَلَائِكَةِ، وَأَمَرَهُمْ بِالسُّجُودِ لَهُ.

وَإِنَّمَا شَرُفَ الْعِلْمُ؛ بِكَوْنِهِ وَسِيلَةً إِلَى الْبِرِّ وَالتَّقْوَىٰ؛ الَّذِي يَسْتَحِقُّ بِهَا الْمَرْءُ الْكَرَامَةَ عِنْدَ اللَّهِ، وَالسَّعَادَةَ الْأَبَدِيَّةَ، كَمَا قِيلَ لِمُحَمَّدِ بْنِ الْحَسَنِ رَحْمَةُ اللَّهِ عَلَيْهِمَا:

تَعَلَّمْ فَإِنَّ الْعِلْمَ زَيْنٌ لِأَهْلِهِ ... وَفَضْلٌ وَعُنْوَانٌ لِكُلِّ الْمَحَامِدِ
وَكُنْ مُسْتَفِيدًا كُلَّ يَوْمٍ زِيَادَةً ... مِنَ الْعِلْمِ وَاسْبَحْ فِي بُحُورِ الْفَوَائِدِ
تَفَقَّهْ فَإِنَّ الْفِقْهَ أَفْضَلُ قَائِدٍ ... إِلَى الْبِرِّ وَالتَّقْوَى وَأَعْدَلُ قَاصِدٍ
هُوَ الْعَلَمُ الْهَادِي إِلَى سُنَنِ الْهُدَى ... هُوَ الْحِصْنُ يُنْجِي مِنْ جَمِيعِ الشَّدَائِدِ
فَإِنَّ فَقِيهًا وَاحِدًا مُتَوَرِّعًا ... أَشَدُّ عَلَى الشَّيْطَانِ مِنْ أَلْفِ عَابِدٍ

وَالْعِلْمُ وَسِيلَةٌ إِلَىٰ مَعْرِفَةِ: الْكِبْرِ، وَالتَّوَاضُعِ، وَالْأُلْفَةِ، وَالْعِفَّةِ، وَالْإِسْرَافِ، وَالتَّقْتِيرِ، وَغَيْرِهَا، وَكَذَلِكَ فِي سَائِرِ الْأَخْلَاقِ؛ نَحْوُ: الْجُودِ، وَالْبُخْلِ، وَالْجُبْنِ، وَالْجَرَاءَةِ.

فَإِنَّ الْكِبْرَ، وَالْبُخْلَ، وَالْجُبْنَ، وَالْإِسْرَافَ حَرَامٌ، وَلَا يُمْكِنُ التَّحَرُّزُ عَنْهَا إِلَّا بِعِلْمِهَا، وَعِلْمِ مَا يُضَادُّهَا، فَيُفْتَرَضُ عَلَىٰ كُلِّ إِنْسَانٍ عِلْمُهَا.

وَقَدْ صَنَّفَ السَّيِّدُ الْإِمَامُ الْأَجَلُ الْأُسْتَاذُ الشَّهِيدُ نَاصِرُ الدِّينِ أَبُو الْقَاسِمِ كِتَابًا فِي «الْأَخْلَاقِ»، وَنِعْمَ مَا صَنَّفَ، فَيَجِبُ عَلَىٰ كُلِّ مُسْلِمٍ حِفْظُهَا.

stances, it is a communal obligation (*farḍ kifāya*); if some individuals fulfil it within a community, the obligation is lifted from the rest. However, if no one in that community takes on this responsibility, all share in the sin. Therefore, the imam must command the people of the community to undertake it and compel them to do so.

It is said that the knowledge of what pertains to oneself in all situations is akin to food, which everyone must have. The knowledge relevant to specific times is like medicine, needed only at certain occasions. The knowledge of astronomy is comparable to illness; learning it is prohibited, as it is harmful and provides no benefit, and escaping from Allah's decree and destiny is impossible.

Thus, every Muslim should engage at all times in the remembrance of Allah, supplication, humility, recitation of the Qur'an, charitable acts that ward off calamities, and prayer. They should ask Allah for forgiveness and wellness in this world and the Hereafter, so that Allah protects them from calamities and afflictions. Indeed, whoever is granted the ability to supplicate will not be deprived of a response. If a calamity is destined to befall them, it will surely happen, but Allah may ease it for them and grant them patience through the blessings of their supplications.

It is permissible to learn about astronomy only to the extent necessary for determining the qiblah and the times for prayer. However, studying medicine is permissible, as it is a means among other means. Thus, acquiring knowledge of it is allowed, just like all other means [of beneficial knowledge].

The Prophet ﷺ sought medical treatment, and it has been reported that Imām al-Shāfiʿī ؓ stated: "There are two kinds of knowledge: the knowledge of jurisprudence for religious matters and the knowledge of medicine for bodily matters. Anything beyond that is merely the chatter of a gathering."

As for the explanation of knowledge: It is an accident through

وَأَمَّا حِفْظُ مَا يَقَعُ فِي الْأَحَايِينِ فَفَرْضٌ عَلَىٰ سَبِيلِ الْكِفَايَةِ، إِذَا قَامَ بِهِ الْبَعْضُ فِي بَلْدَةٍ سَقَطَ عَنِ الْبَاقِينَ، فَإِنْ لَمْ يَكُنْ فِي الْبَلْدَةِ مَنْ يَقُومُ بِهِ اشْتَرَكُوا جَمِيعًا فِي الْمَأْثَمِ، فَيَجِبُ عَلَى الْإِمَامِ أَنْ يَأْمُرَهُمْ بِذَلِكَ، وَيُجْبِرَ أَهْلَ الْبَلْدَةِ عَلَىٰ ذَلِكَ.

قِيلَ: إِنَّ عِلْمَ مَا يَقَعُ عَلَى نَفْسِهِ فِي جَمِيعِ الْأَحْوَالِ بِمَنْزِلَةِ الطَّعَامِ لَا بُدَّ لِكُلِّ وَاحِدٍ مِنْ ذَلِكَ، وَعِلْمُ مَا يَقَعُ فِي الْأَحَايِينِ بِمَنْزِلَةِ الدَّوَاءِ يُحْتَاجُ إِلَيْهِ فِي بَعْضِ الْأَوْقَاتِ.

وَعِلْمُ النُّجُومِ بِمَنْزِلَةِ الْمَرَضِ، فَتَعَلُّمُهُ حَرَامٌ ؛ لِأَنَّهُ يَضُرُّ وَلَا يَنْفَعُ، وَالْهَرَبُ عَنْ قَضَاءِ اللَّهِ تَعَالَىٰ وَقَدَرِهِ غَيْرُ مُمْكِنٍ.

فَيَنْبَغِي لِكُلِّ مُسْلِمٍ أَنْ يَشْتَغِلَ فِي جَمِيعِ أَوْقَاتِهِ بِذِكْرِ اللَّهِ تَعَالَىٰ وَالدُّعَاءِ، وَالتَّضَرُّعِ، وَقِرَاءَةِ الْقُرْآنِ، وَالصَّدَقَاتِ الدَّافِعَةِ لِلْبَلَاءِ، وَالصَّلَاةِ، وَيَسْأَلَ اللَّهَ تَعَالَى الْعَفْوَ وَالْعَافِيَةَ فِي الدُّنْيَا وَالْآخِرَةِ؛ لِيَصُونَ اللَّهُ عَنْهُ تَعَالَى الْبَلَاءَ وَالْآفَاتِ، فَإِنَّ مَنْ رُزِقَ الدُّعَاءَ لَمْ يُحْرَمِ الْإِجَابَةَ، فَإِنْ كَانَ الْبَلَاءُ مُقَدَّرًا يُصِيبُهُ لَا مَحَالَةَ؛ وَلَكِنْ يُيَسِّرُهُ اللَّهُ عَلَيْهِ وَيَرْزُقُهُ الصَّبْرَ بِبَرَكَةِ الدُّعَاءِ.

اللَّهُمَّ إِلَّا إِذَا تَعَلَّمَ مِنَ النُّجُومِ قَدْرَ مَا يَعْرِفُ بِهِ الْقِبْلَةَ، وَأَوْقَاتَ الصَّلَاةِ، فَيَجُوزُ ذَلِكَ، وَأَمَّا تَعَلُّمُ عِلْمِ الطِّبِّ فَيَجُوزُ؛ لِأَنَّهُ سَبَبٌ مِنَ الْأَسْبَابِ، فَيَجُوزُ تَعَلُّمُهُ كَسَائِرِ الْأَسْبَابِ.

وَقَدْ تَدَاوَى النَّبِيُّ عَلَيْهِ السَّلَامُ، وَقَدْ حُكِيَ عَنِ الشَّافِعِي رَحْمَةُ اللَّهِ عَلَيْهِ أَنَّهُ قَالَ: الْعِلْمُ عِلْمَانِ: عِلْمُ الْفِقْهِ لِلْأَدْيَانِ، وَعِلْمُ الطِّبِّ لِلْأَبْدَانِ،

which the mentioned is manifest for the one with whom it is established – as it really is.[1] Jurisprudence (*fiqh*) refers to the understanding of the subtleties of knowledge along with the type of treatment required.

Abū Ḥanīfah ﷺ said: "Fiqh is the knowledge of what pertains to oneself – what is due to it and what it owes." He also stated: "Knowledge is only for the purpose of action, and acting upon it means forsaking the immediate for the delayed."

Thus, a person should not neglect understanding what benefits one and what harms one in both this world and the Hereafter. One should seek out what is beneficial and avoid what is harmful so that one's intellect and knowledge do not serve as a proof against one, leading to increased punishment. We seek refuge in Allah from His wrath and punishment.

There are numerous verses and authentic reports regarding the merits and virtues of knowledge, but we have refrained from detailing them to avoid lengthening this text.

---

(1) Translator: Knowledge is technically described – by Muslim theologians – as an accident, meaning an attribute, through which anything mentioned is manifest – meaning the image of which is imprinted within the mind – as it really is. As it really is, here, means that this is not a *khayāl*, a mere supposition, rather this image within the mind, this knowledge, corresponds to the thing itself in extramental existence.

وَمَا وَرَاءَ ذَلِكَ بُلْغَةُ مَجْلِسٍ.

وَأَمَّا تَفْسِيرُ الْعِلْمِ: فَهُوَ صِفَةٌ يَتَحَلَّى بِهَا الْمَذْكُورُ لِمَنْ قَامَتْ هِيَ بِهِ كَمَا هُوَ.

وَالْفِقْهُ: مَعْرِفَةُ دَقَائِقِ الْعِلْمِ مَعَ نَوْعِ عِلَاجٍ.

قَالَ أَبُو حَنِيفَةَ رَحْمَةُ اللَّهِ عَلَيْهِ: الْفِقْهُ مَعْرِفَةُ النَّفْسِ مَا لَهَا وَمَا عَلَيْهَا.

وَقَالَ: مَا الْعِلْمُ إِلَّا لِلْعَمَلِ بِهِ، وَالْعَمَلُ بِهِ تَرْكُ الْعَاجِلِ لِلْآجِلِ.

فَيَنْبَغِي لِلْإِنْسَانِ أَلَّا يَغْفَلَ عَنْ نَفْسِهِ مَا يَنْفَعُهَا وَمَا يَضُرُّهَا فِي أَوَّلِهَا وَآخِرِهَا، وَيَسْتَجْلِبُ مَا يَنْفَعُهَا وَيَجْتَنِبُ عَمَّا يَضُرُّهَا كَيْ لَا يَكُونَ عَقْلُهُ وَعِلْمُهُ حُجَّةً عَلَيْهِ فَيَزْدَادُ عُقُوبَةً، نَعُوذُ بِاللَّهِ مِنْ سَخَطِهِ وَعِقَابِهِ.

وَقَدْ وَرَدَ فِي مَنَاقِبِ الْعِلْمِ وَفَضَائِلِهِ آيَاتٌ وَأَخْبَارٌ صَحِيحَةٌ مَشْهُورَةٌ لَمْ نَشْتَغِلْ بِذِكْرِهَا كَيْ لَا يَطُولَ الْكِتَابُ.

It is essential for a learner to have the right intention during the time of acquiring knowledge, for intention is the foundation of all actions, as the Prophet Muhammad ﷺ said: "Indeed, actions are judged by intentions". It is a sound Hadith from the Messenger ﷺ. How many actions appear as worldly deeds but, with a good intention, transform into acts of the Hereafter? And how many actions seem to be for the Hereafter but, due to bad intentions, become actions of this world?

The learner should intend, in seeking knowledge, to please Allah and attain the Hereafter, to remove ignorance from himself and from others, and to revive the religion and uphold Islam – for the survival of Islam is through knowledge, and one cannot truly practice piety and devotion while remaining in ignorance.

The esteemed *shaykh* and imam Burhān al-Dīn, the author of *Al-Hidāyah*, recited for us:

*A great corruption is a shameless scholar,*
*And greater than him is a pious ignoramus.*
*Both are a great trial for the world*
*For those who hold onto their faith through them.*

One should also intend to express gratitude for the blessing of intellect and the health of the body, and not to seek the attention of others, nor to attract the fleeting gains of this world, nor to gain honour with the sultan or others.

Muhammad ibn al-Ḥasan said: "If all the people were my slaves, I would free them and renounce my allegiance to them." This is because one who finds the pleasure of knowledge and acts upon it rarely desires what is with people.

The esteemed *shaykh* and imam Qiwām al-Dīn Ḥammād ibn Ibrāhīm al-Anṣārī recited on behalf of Abū Ḥanīfah:

*Whoever seeks knowledge for the Hereafter*

## فَصلٌ فِي النِّيَّةِ فِي حَالِ التَّعلُّمِ

ثُمَّ لَا بُدَّ لَهُ مِنَ النِّيَّةِ فِي زَمَانِ تَعَلُّمِ الْعِلْمِ؛ إِذِ النِّيَّةُ هِيَ الْأَصْلُ فِي جَمِيعِ الْأَفْعَالِ لِقَوْلِهِ عَلَيْهِ السَّلَامُ: «إِنَّمَا الْأَعْمَالُ بِالنِّيَاتِ». حَدِيثٌ صَحِيحٌ عَنِ الرَّسُولِ ﷺ.

كَمْ مِنْ عَمَلٍ يُتَصَوَّرُ بِصُورَةِ عَمَلِ الدُّنْيَا، ثُمَّ يَصِيرُ بِحُسنِ النِّيَّةِ مِنْ أَعْمَالِ الْآخِرَةِ، وَكَمْ مِنْ عَمَلٍ يُتَصَوَّرُ بِصُورَةِ عَمَلِ الْآخِرَةِ ثُمَّ يَصِيرُ مِنْ أَعْمَالِ الدُّنْيَا بِسُوءِ النِّيَّةِ.

وَيَنْبَغِي أَنْ يَنْوِيَ الْمُتَعَلِّمُ بِطَلَبِ الْعِلْمِ رِضَاءَ اللهِ وَالدَّارَ الْآخِرَةَ، وَإِزَالَةَ الْجَهْلِ عَنْ نَفْسِهِ، وَعَنْ سَائِرِ الْجُهَّالِ، وَإِحْيَاءَ الدِّينِ وَإِبْقَاءَ الْإِسْلَامِ؛ فَإِنَّ بَقَاءَ الْإِسْلَامِ بِالْعِلْمِ، وَلَا يَصِحُّ الزُّهْدُ وَالتَّقْوَىٰ مَعَ الْجَهْلِ. وَأَنْشَدَنَا الشَّيْخُ الْإِمَامُ الْأَجَلُّ الْأُسْتَاذُ بُرْهَانُ الدِّينِ صَاحِبُ «الهِدَايَةِ» لِبَعْضِهِمْ:

فَسَادٌ كَبِيرٌ عَالِمٌ مُتَهَتِّكٌ ... وَأَكْبَرُ مِنْهُ جَاهِلٌ مُتَنَسِّكُ

هُمَا فِتْنَةٌ لِلْعَالَمِينَ عَظِيمَةٌ ... لِمَنْ بِهِمَا فِي دِينِهِ يَتَمَسَّكُ

وَيَنْوِي بِهِ: الشُّكْرَ عَلَىٰ نِعْمَةِ الْعَقْلِ، وَصِحَّةِ الْبَدَنِ، وَلَا يَنْوِي بِهِ إِقْبَالَ النَّاسِ عَلَيْهِ، وَلَا اسْتِجْلَابَ حُطَامِ الدُّنْيَا، وَالْكَرَامَةَ عِنْدَ السُّلْطَانِ وَغَيْرِهِ. وَقَالَ مُحَمَّدُ بْنُ الْحَسَنِ رَحْمَةُ اللهِ عَلَيْهِمَا: لَوْ كَانَ النَّاسُ كُلُّهُمْ عَبِيدِي لَأَعْتَقْتُهُمْ وَتَبَرَّأْتُ مِنْ وَلَائِهِمْ. وَذَلِكَ؛ لِأَنَّ مَنْ وَجَدَ لَذَّةَ الْعِلْمِ وَالْعَمَلِ بِهِ، قَلَّمَا يَرْغَبُ فِيمَا عِنْدَ النَّاسِ.

*Gains a blessing from guidance.*
*Oh the loss of those who seek it*
*To attain the favour from the servants!*

Except if one seeks status for the purpose of enjoining what is right and forbidding what is wrong, implementing the truth, and honouring the religion, not for oneself or one's desires; this is permissible to the extent that it establishes enjoining what is right and forbidding what is wrong.

It is important for the seeker of knowledge to reflect on this, for he learns knowledge with great effort, so he should not waste it on the trivial and fleeting matters of this world. The Prophet ﷺ said: "Beware of this world, for, by the One in Whose hand is the soul of Muhammad, it is indeed more enchanting than the magic of Ḥārūt and Mārūt."

*This world is less than trivial,*
*And its lover is more humiliated than the humiliated.*
*It deafens some with its sorcery and blinds others,*
*So they wander confused without guidance.*

The seeker of knowledge should not humiliate himself by craving what is beyond his reach, and he should guard against anything that leads to the humiliation of knowledge and its people. He should be humble, for humility lies between arrogance and humiliation, and chastity is similar; this is well documented in *The Book of Ethics*.

The esteemed *shaykh* and imam the honoured Rukn al-Dīn al-Maʿrūf recited to me poetry for himself:

*Indeed, humility is one of the traits of the pious,*
*And with it, the righteous ascend to great heights.*
*Among the wonders is the astonishment of one who is ignorant;*
*Is he in a state of happiness or misery?*
*How will his life end or his soul depart*
*On the day of separation, whether in decline or ascent?*
*Greatness belongs to our Lord as a unique attribute;*

أَنْشَدَنَا الشَّيْخُ الإِمَامُ الأَجَلُّ الأُسْتَاذُ قِوَامُ الدِّينِ حَمَّادُ بْنُ إِبْرَاهِيمَ بْنُ إِسْمَاعِيلَ الصَّفَّارُ الأَنْصَارِيُّ إِمْلَاءً لِأَبِي حَنِيفَةَ رَحْمَةُ اللهِ عَلَيْهِ:

مَنْ طَلَبَ العِلْمَ لِلْمَعَادِ فَازَ بِفَضْلٍ مِنَ الرَّشَادِ
فَيَا لِخُسْرَانِ طَالِبِيهِ لِنَيْلِ فَضْلٍ مِنَ العِبَادِ

اللَّهُمَّ إِلَّا إِذَا طَلَبَ الجَاهَ لِلْأَمْرِ بِالْمَعْرُوفِ وَالنَّهْيِ عَنِ الْمُنْكَرِ، وَتَنْفِيذِ الحَقِّ، وَإِعزَازِ الدِّينِ لَا لِنَفْسِهِ وَهَوَاهُ، فَيَجُوزُ ذَلِكَ بِقَدْرِ مَا يُقِيمُ بِهِ الْأَمْرَ بِالْمَعْرُوفِ وَالنَّهْيَ عَنِ الْمُنْكَرِ.

وَيَنْبَغِي لِطَالِبِ الْعِلْمِ: أَنْ يَتَفَكَّرَ فِي ذَلِكَ، فَإِنَّهُ يَتَعَلَّمُ الْعِلْمَ بِجُهْدٍ كَثِيرٍ، فَلَا يَصْرِفُهُ إِلَى الدُّنْيَا الْحَقِيرَةِ الْقَلِيلَةِ الْفَانِيَةِ.

قَالَ النَّبِيُّ ﷺ: «اتَّقُوا الدُّنْيَا، فَوَالَّذِي نَفْسُ مُحَمَّدٍ بِيَدِهِ إِنَّهَا لَأَسْحَرُ مِنْ هَارُوتَ وَمَارُوتَ».

هِيَ الدُّنْيَا أَقَلُّ مِنَ الْقَلِيلِ وَعَاشِقُهَا أَذَلُّ مِنَ الذَّلِيلِ
تُصِمُّ بِسِحْرِهَا قَوْمًا وَتُعْمِي فَهُمْ مُتَحَيِّرُونَ بِلَا دَلِيلِ

وَيَنْبَغِي لِطَالِبِ الْعِلْمِ أَلَّا يُذِلَّ نَفْسَهُ بِالطَّمَعِ فِي غَيْرِ الْمَطْمَعِ، وَيَحْتَرِزَ عَمَّا فِيهِ مَذَلَّةُ الْعِلْمِ وَأَهْلِهِ.

وَيَكُونَ مُتَوَاضِعًا، وَالتَّوَاضُعُ بَيْنَ التَّكَبُّرِ وَالذِّلَّةِ، وَالْعِفَّةُ كَذَلِكَ، وَيُعْرَفُ ذَلِكَ فِي كِتَابِ «الْأَخْلَاقِ».

أَنْشَدَنِي الشَّيْخُ الْإِمَامُ الْأُسْتَاذُ رُكْنُ الدِّينِ الْمَعْرُوفُ بِـ «الْأَدِيبِ الْمُخْتَارِ» شِعْرًا لِنَفْسِهِ:

*So avoid it and be conscious of Him.*

Abū Ḥanīfah ﵀ said to his companions: "Honour your turbans and widen your sleeves." He said this so that knowledge and its people would not be taken lightly.

The seeker of knowledge should strive to acquire *The Book of Counsel,* which Abū Ḥanīfah ﵀ wrote for Yūsuf ibn Khālid al-Samtī for when he returned to his people. This book is essential for anyone pursuing knowledge.

Our esteemed teacher, the Shaykh al-Islām, Burḥān al-Dīn ʿAlī ibn Abī Bakr (may Allah sanctify his noble soul) commanded me to write this [work] upon my return to my homeland, and I did so. It is imperative for the teacher and the mufti to refer to this in their dealings with people, and success is from Allah.

إِنَّ التَّوَاضُعَ مِنْ خِصَالِ الْمُتَّقِي  وَبِهِ التَّقِيُّ إِلَى الْمَعَالِي يَرْتَقِي
وَمِنَ الْعَجَائِبِ عُجْبُ مَنْ هُوَ جَاهِلٌ  فِي حَالِهِ أَهُوَ السَّعِيدُ أَمِ الشَّقِي
أَمْ كَيْفَ يُخْتَمُ عُمْرُهُ أَوْ رُوحُهُ  يَوْمَ النَّوَى مُتَسَفِّلٌ أَوْ مُرْتَقِي
وَالْكِبْرِيَاءُ لِرَبِّنَا صِفَةٌ لَهُ  مَخْصُوصَةٌ فَتَجَنَّبَنْهَا وَاتَّقِي

قَالَ أَبُو حَنِيفَةَ رَحْمَةُ اللهِ عَلَيْهِ لِأَصْحَابِهِ: «عَظِّمُوا عَمَائِمَكُمْ، وَوَسِّعُوا أَكْمَامَكُمْ».

وَإِنَّمَا قَالَ ذَلِكَ لِئَلَّا يُسْتَخَفَّ بِالْعِلْمِ وَأَهْلِهِ.

وَيَنْبَغِي لِطَالِبِ الْعِلْمِ أَنْ يُحَصِّلَ «كِتَابَ الْوَصِيَّةِ» الَّتِي كَتَبَهَا أَبُو حَنِيفَةَ رَحْمَةُ اللَّهِ عَلَيْهِ لِيُوسُفَ بْنِ خَالِدِ السَّمْتِي عِنْدَ الرُّجُوعِ إِلَى أَهْلِهِ، يَجِدُهُ مَنْ يَطْلُبُ الْعِلْمَ.

وَقَدْ كَانَ أُسْتَاذُنَا شَيْخُ الْإِسْلَامِ بُرْهَانُ الدِّينِ عَلِيُّ بْنُ أَبِي بَكْرٍ - قَدَّسَ اللَّهُ رُوحَهُ الْعَزِيزَ - أَمَرَنِي بِكِتَابَتِهِ عِنْدَ الرُّجُوعِ إِلَى بَلَدِي فَكَتَبْتُهُ، وَلَا بُدَّ لِلْمُدَرِّسِ وَالْمُفْتِي فِي مُعَامَلَاتِ النَّاسِ مِنْهُ، وَبِاللَّهِ التَّوْفِيقُ.

## CHOOSING KNOWLEDGE, THE TEACHER, THE COMPANION, AND STEADFASTNESS

A student of knowledge should choose the best from every field of knowledge and select what he needs for his religion at the present time, as well as what he will need in the future.

He should prioritise the knowledge of *tawḥīd* and understanding, recognising Allah, the Exalted, through evidence. While the belief of the follower may be correct in our view, he still bears sin for neglecting to seek proof.

He should prefer the ancient teachings over modern innovations. It is said: "Adhere to the ancient and avoid the newly innovated", and beware of engaging in the disputes that have emerged after the passing of the great scholars. Such disputes distract from true understanding, waste time, and foster enmity, as it is one of the signs of the Hour and a consequence of the decline of knowledge and jurisprudence, as mentioned in the Hadith.

As for choosing a teacher, one should select the most knowledgeable, pious, and senior among them. Abū Ḥanīfah ﷺ chose Ḥammād ibn Abī Sulaymān after careful reflection, stating: "I found him to be a venerable, wise, and patient man in matters." He said: "I remained steadfast with Ḥammād ibn Abī Sulaymān, and I flourished."

Abū Ḥanīfah ﷺ narrated that he heard a wise man from Samarkand say: "One of the students of knowledge consulted me about seeking knowledge, as he had resolved to go to Bukhara to pursue it." Likewise, one should seek counsel in every matter. Indeed, Allah, the Exalted, commanded His Messenger ﷺ to consult in affairs, and there was no one more discerning than him, yet he was commanded to consult, often discussing matters with his companions, even regarding household needs.

ʿAlī (may Allah honour his face) said: "No person has ever

## فَصْلٌ فِي اخْتِيَارِ الْعِلْمِ، وَالْأُسْتَاذِ، وَالشَّرِيكِ، وَالثَّبَاتِ

وَيَنْبَغِي لِطَالِبِ الْعِلْمِ أَنْ يَخْتَارَ مِنْ كُلِّ عِلْمٍ أَحْسَنَهُ، وَمَا يَحْتَاجُ إِلَيْهِ فِي أَمْرِ دِينِهِ فِي الْحَالِ، ثُمَّ مَا يَحْتَاجُ إِلَيْهِ فِي الْمَآلِ.

وَيُقَدِّمُ عِلْمَ التَّوْحِيدِ وَالْمَعْرِفَةِ، وَيَعْرِفُ اللهَ تَعَالَىٰ بِالدَّلِيلِ؛ فَإِنَّ إِيمَانَ الْمُقَلِّدِ وَإِنْ كَانَ صَحِيحًا عِنْدَنَا؛ لكِنْ يَكُونُ آثِمًا بِتَرْكِ الاسْتِدْلَالِ.

وَيَخْتَارُ الْعَتِيقَ دُونَ الْمُحْدَثَاتِ، قَالُوا: عَلَيْكُمْ بِالْعَتِيقِ وَإِيَّاكُمْ وَالْمُحْدَثَاتِ، وَإِيَّاكَ أَنْ تَشْتَغِلَ بِهَذَا الْجِدَالِ الَّذِي ظَهَرَ بَعْدَ انْقِرَاضِ الْأَكَابِرِ مِنَ الْعُلَمَاءِ، فَإِنَّهُ يُبْعِدُ عَنِ الْفِقْهِ وَيُضَيِّعُ الْعُمُرَ وَيُورِثُ الْوَحْشَةَ وَالْعَدَاوَةَ، وَهُوَ مِنْ أَشْرَاطِ السَّاعَةِ وَارْتِفَاعِ الْعِلْمِ وَالْفِقْهِ، كَذَا وَرَدَ فِي الْحَدِيثِ.

أَمَّا اخْتِيَارُ الْأُسْتَاذِ فَيَنْبَغِي أَنْ يَخْتَارَ الْأَعْلَمَ وَالْأَوْرَعَ وَالْأَسَنَّ، كَمَا اخْتَارَ أَبُو حَنِيفَةَ رَحْمَةُ اللَّهِ عَلَيْهِ، حَمَّادَ ابْنَ أَبِي سُلَيْمَانَ، بَعْدَ التَّأَمُّلِ وَالتَّفَكُّرِ، وَقَالَ: «وَجَدْتُهُ شَيْخًا وَقُورًا حَلِيمًا صَبُورًا فِي الْأُمُورِ».

وَقَالَ: «ثَبَتُّ عِنْدَ حَمَّادِ ابْنِ أَبِي سُلَيْمَانَ فَنَبَتُّ».

وَقَالَ أَبُو حَنِيفَةَ رَحْمَةُ اللَّهِ عَلَيْهِ: سَمِعْتُ حَكِيمًا مِنْ حُكَمَاءِ سَمَرْقَنْدَ قَالَ: إِنَّ وَاحِدًا مِنْ طَلَبَةِ الْعِلْمِ شَاوَرَنِي فِي طَلَبِ الْعِلْمِ، وَكَانَ قَدْ عَزَمَ عَلَى الذَّهَابِ إِلَى بُخَارَىٰ لِطَلَبِ الْعِلْمِ.

وَهَكَذَا يَنْبَغِي أَنْ يُشَاوِرَ فِي كُلِّ أَمْرٍ، فَإِنَّ اللهَ تَعَالَى أَمَرَ رَسُولَهُ عَلَيْهِ الصَّلَاةُ وَالسَّلَامُ بِالْمُشَاوَرَةِ فِي الْأُمُورِ، وَلَمْ يَكُنْ أَحَدٌ أَفْطَنَ مِنْهُ،

perished due to consultation." It was said: "[There are] a complete man, half a man, and nothing."

The complete man is one who possesses sound judgment and consults the wise. Half a man is one who either has sound judgment but does not consult or consults but lacks sound judgment. And "nothing" refers to someone who neither has sound judgment nor seeks consultation.

Ja'far al-Ṣādiq advised Sufyān al-Thawrī: "Consult those who fear Allah, the Exalted, regarding your affairs." Seeking knowledge is among the highest and most challenging pursuits, and thus consultation in it is of utmost importance and most binding.

Al-Hakīm ﷺ[2] said: "When you go to Bukhara, do not hasten to differ with the imams; rather, stay for two months to contemplate and choose a teacher, for if you go to a scholar and begin with haste, you may not find his teaching pleasing and thus abandon him for another, which will bring no blessing to your learning."

Therefore, reflect for two months when choosing a teacher, and consult so that you do not need to abandon him or turn away from him. This will ensure that your learning is blessed and that you benefit greatly from your knowledge.

Know that patience and steadfastness are fundamental principles in all matters, but they are rare. As it is said:

*Every endeavour to reach the heights requires effort,*
*But steadfastness is rare among men.*

It is said: "Courage is a moment of patience." Thus, one should remain steadfast and patient with a teacher and with a

(2) Translator: Al-Hakīm Abū al-Qāsim Ishāq al-Samarqandī was a Sunni-Hanafi scholar, *qāḍī* (judge), and sage from Transoxania who studied Sufism in Balkh with Abū Bakr al-Warrāq. Some sources describe him as a student of al-Māturīdī (d. 333/944-45) in *fiqh* and *kalām*.

وَمَعَ ذَلِكَ أُمِرَ بِالْمُشَاوَرَةِ، وَكَانَ يُشَاوِرُ أَصْحَابَهُ فِي جَمِيعِ الْأُمُورِ حَتَّىٰ حَوَائِجَ الْبَيْتِ.

قَالَ عَلِيٌّ كَرَّمَ اللهُ وَجْهَهُ : مَا هَلَكَ امْرُؤٌ عَنْ مَشُورَةٍ.

قِيلَ : رَجُلٌ تَامٌّ، وَنِصْفُ رَجُلٍ، وَلَا شَيْءَ؛ فَالرَّجُلُ: مَنْ لَهُ رَأْيٌ صَائِبٌ وَيُشَاوِرُ الْعُقَلَاءَ، وَنِصْفُ رَجُلٍ: مَنْ لَهُ رَأْيٌ صَائِبٌ لَكِنْ لَا يُشَاوِرُ، أَوْ يُشَاوِرُ وَلَكِنْ لَا رَأْيَ لَهُ. وَلَا شَيْءَ: مَنْ لَا رَأْيَ لَهُ وَلَا يُشَاوِرُ.

وَقَالَ جَعْفَرُ الصَّادِقُ لِسُفْيَانَ الثَّوْرِيِّ: «شَاوِرْ فِي أَمْرِكَ الَّذِينَ يَخْشَوْنَ اللَّهَ تَعَالَىٰ».

فَطَلَبُ الْعِلْمِ مِنْ أَعْلَى الْأُمُورِ وَأَصْعَبِهَا، فَكَانَتِ الْمُشَاوَرَةُ فِيهِ أَهَمَّ وَأَوْجَبَ. قَالَ الْحَكِيمُ رَحْمَةُ اللَّهِ عَلَيْهِ: إِذَا ذَهَبْتَ إِلَىٰ بُخَارَىٰ فَلَا تَعْجَلْ فِي الاخْتِلَافِ إِلَى الْأَئِمَّةِ، وَامْكُثْ شَهْرَيْنِ حَتَّى تَتَأَمَّلَ وَتَخْتَارَ أُسْتَاذًا، فَإِنَّكَ إِنْ ذَهَبْتَ إِلَىٰ عَالِمٍ وَبَدَأْتَ بِالسَّبَقِ عِنْدَهُ فَرُبَّمَا لَا يُعْجِبُكَ دَرْسُهُ فَتَتْرُكُهُ فَتَذْهَبُ إِلَى آخَرٍ، فَلَا يُبَارَكُ لَكَ فِي التَّعَلُّمِ. فَتَأَمَّلْ فِي شَهْرَيْنِ فِي اخْتِيَارِ الْأُسْتَاذِ، وَشَاوِرْ حَتَّىٰ لَا تَحْتَاجَ إِلَىٰ تَرْكِهِ وَالْإِعْرَاضِ عَنْهُ؛ فَتَثْبُتَ عِنْدَهُ حَتَّى يَكُونَ تَعَلُّمُكَ مُبَارَكًا وَتَنْتَفِعَ بِعِلْمِكَ كَثِيرًا.

وَاعْلَمْ بِأَنَّ الصَّبْرَ وَالثَّبَاتَ أَصْلٌ كَبِيرٌ فِي جَمِيعِ الْأُمُورِ؛ وَلَكِنَّهُ عَزِيزٌ، كَمَا قِيلَ:

book, ensuring that one does not leave it incomplete, and with a discipline until one masters it before engaging in another. One should remain in a locality until there is no necessity to move to another, for all of this disperses one's focus, occupies the heart, wastes time, and burdens the teacher.

One should also practise patience against the craving of one's soul and desire. The poet said:

*Indeed, desire is the very essence of degradation,*
*And every passion is a captive to degradation.*

One should endure trials and tribulations. It is said: "The treasures of blessings are upon the scales of trials."

It has been reported, and it is said to be attributed to ʿAlī ibn Abī Ṭālib (may Allah honour his face):

*You will not attain knowledge except through six things,*
*I will inform you of their totality clearly:*
*Intelligence, eagerness, perseverance, eloquence,*
*Guidance from a teacher, and a long duration.*

As for choosing a companion, one should select the industrious, the pious, and the person of a straightforward and understanding nature, while avoiding the lazy, the negligent, the indecisive, the corrupt, and the disruptive. The poet said:

*Do not ask about a person; rather observe his companion,*
*For the companion leads one by example.*
*If he is of evil character, quickly distance yourself from him,*
*And if he is of good character, associate with him and you will be guided.*

I have recited another poem:

*Do not accompany the lazy in their endeavours;*
*How often the righteous are corrupted by others.*
*The influence of the dullard spreads quickly,*
*Like embers placed in ash, they are extinguished.*

لِكُلٍّ إِلَى شَأْوِ الْعُلَا حَرَكَاتُ        وَلَكِنْ عَزِيزٌ فِي الرِّجَالِ ثَبَاتُ

قِيلَ: الشَّجَاعَةُ صَبْرُ سَاعَةٍ. فَيَنْبَغِي أَنْ يَثْبُتَ وَيَصْبِرَ عَلَىٰ أُسْتَاذٍ وَعَلَىٰ كِتَابٍ حَتَّى لَا يَتْرُكَهُ أَبْتَرَ، وَعَلَىٰ فَنٍّ حَتَّىٰ لَا يَشْتَغِلَ بِفَنٍّ آخَرَ قَبْلَ أَنْ يُتْقِنَ الْأَوَّلَ، وَعَلَىٰ بَلَدٍ حَتَّىٰ لَا يَنْتَقِلَ إِلَىٰ بَلَدٍ آخَرَ مِنْ غَيْرِ ضَرُورَةٍ، فَإِنَّ ذَلِكَ كُلَّهُ يُفَرِّقُ الْأُمُورَ وَيُشْغِلُ الْقَلْبَ وَيُضَيِّعُ الْأَوْقَاتَ وَيُؤْذِي الْمُعَلِّمَ. وَيَنْبَغِي أَنْ يَصْبِرَ عَمَّا تُرِيدُهُ نَفْسُهُ وَهَوَاهُ. قَالَ الشَّاعِرُ:

إِنَّ الْهَوَىٰ لَهُوَ الْهَوَانُ بِعَيْنِهِ        وَصَرِيعُ كُلِّ هَوًى صَرِيعُ هَوَانِ

وَيَصْبِرَ عَلَى الْمِحَنِ وَالْبَلِيَّاتِ. قِيلَ: «خَزَائِنُ الْمِنَنِ، عَلَىٰ قَنَاطِيرِ الْمِحَنِ». **وَلَقَدْ** أُنْشِدْتُ، وَقِيلَ: إِنَّهُ لِعَلِيِّ بْنِ أَبِي طَالِبٍ كَرَّمَ اللَّهُ وَجْهَهُ:

أَلَا لَنْ تَنَالَ الْعِلْمَ إِلَّا بِسِتَّةٍ        سَأُنْبِيكَ عَنْ مَجْمُوعِهَا بِبَيَانِ
ذَكَاءٌ وَحِرْصٌ وَاصْطِبَارٌ وَبُلْغَةٌ        وَإِرْشَادُ أُسْتَاذٍ وَطُولُ زَمَانِ

وَأَمَّا اخْتِيَارُ الشَّرِيكِ فَيَنْبَغِي أَنْ يَخْتَارَ الْمُجِدَّ وَالْوَرِعَ وَصَاحِبَ الطَّبْعِ الْمُسْتَقِيمِ الْمُتَفَهِّمِ، وَيَفِرَّ مِنَ الْكَسْلَانِ وَالْمُعَطِّلِ وَالْمِكْثَارِ وَالْمُفْسِدِ وَالْفَتَّانِ، قَالَ الشَّاعِرُ:

عَنِ الْمَرْءِ لَا تَسَلْ وَأَبْصِرْ قَرِينَهُ        فَإِنَّ الْقَرِينَ بِالْمُقَارِنِ يَقْتَدِي
فَإِنْ كَانَ ذَا شَرٍّ فَجَانِبْهُ سُرْعَةً        وَإِنْ كَانَ ذَا خَيْرٍ فَقَارِنْهُ تَهْتَدِي

وَأُنْشِدْتُ شِعْرًا آخَرَ:

لَا تَصْحَبِ الْكَسْلَانَ فِي حَالَاتِهِ        كَمْ صَالِحٍ بِفَسَادِ آخَرَ يَفْسُدُ

The Prophet ﷺ said: "Every newborn is born on the *fiṭrah* of Islam, except that his parents make him a Jew, a Christian, or a Magian."[3] And it is said in wisdom in Persian:

*Barbād was worse than Marbād,*
*By the truth of the Pure Essence of Allah, the Self-Sufficient.*
*Barbād hastened towards the abyss of Hell,*
*While the righteous and virtuous ascended to the Blissful Garden.*[4]

It is said:

*If you seek knowledge and its people*
*Or a witness to speak of what is hidden,*
*Then reflect upon the land through its names*
*And assess a companion by his companion.*

---

(3) *Sahih Muslim*, 2659a.

(4) Translator: These verses contrast two archetypal figures – Barbād and Marbād – to convey a moral lesson: Barbād represents negative influence or bad companionship, leading one towards misguidance and, ultimately, punishment (symbolised by Hell). Marbād symbolises positive influence or good companionship, guiding one towards righteousness and reward (symbolised by the Blissful Garden or Paradise). These lines are often cited in classical Islamic literature to highlight the profound impact of one's associates on their moral and spiritual trajectory. They serve as a reminder to choose companions wisely, as they can lead one towards salvation or perdition.

عَدْوَى الْبَلِيدِ إِلَى الْجَلِيدِ سَرِيعَةٌ كَالْجَمْرِ يُوضَعُ فِي الرَّمَادِ فَيُخْمَدُ

قَالَ النَّبِيُّ ﷺ: «كُلُّ مَوْلُودٍ يُولَدُ عَلَىٰ فِطْرَةِ الإِسْلَامِ، إِلَّا أَنَّ أَبَوَاهُ يُهَوِّدَانِهِ وَيُنَصِّرَانِهِ وَيُمَجِّسَانِهِ»، الْحَدِيث.

وَيُقَالُ فِي الْحِكْمَةِ بِالْفَارِسِيَّةِ:

بَارِبَدْ بَدْتَرْ بُودَ أَزْمَارِبَدْ بِحَقِّ ذَاتِ بَاكَ اللّٰهِ الصَّمَدْ
بَارِبَدْ ازْدترا سُوَى جَحِيمْ بَارَ نيكوكير نابي نَعِيم

وَقِيلَ:

إِنْ كُنْتَ تَبْغِي الْعِلْمَ وَأَهْلَهُ أَوْ شَاهِدًا يُخْبِرُ عَنْ غَائِبِ
فَاعْتَبِرِ الْأَرْضَ بِأَسْمَائِهَا وَاعْتَبِرِ الصَّاحِبَ بِالصَّاحِبِ

Know that a student of knowledge cannot attain or benefit from knowledge except by honouring knowledge and its people, and by respecting and revering his teachers.

It is said: "No one reaches their goal except through reverence, and no one falls except by disregarding respect."

Another saying goes: "Respect is better than obedience." Consider that a person does not become a disbeliever through disobedience but rather through trivialising it and disregarding its sanctity.

Part of honouring knowledge is honouring the teacher. ʿAlī said: "I am the servant of whoever teaches me even a single letter – if he wishes, he can sell me, if he wishes, he can enslave me, and if he wishes, he can set me free."

A poem was recited about this:

*I saw the most deserving right to be the right of the teacher,*
*Most obligatory to preserve for every Muslim.*
*Truly, he deserves to be honoured with a gift*
*Of a thousand dirhams for teaching just one letter.*

For whoever teaches you a single letter that you need in your religion is your father in faith.

Our master, the eminent *shaykh*, Ṣadr al-Dīn al-Shirāzī would say that his teachers used to say: "If someone wants his son to become a scholar, he should welcome and honour traveling scholars, feed them, and give them something. If his son does not become a scholar, his grandson will."

Among the ways of respecting the teacher are:

- Not walking ahead of him.
- Not sitting in his place.
- Not speaking without his permission.
- Not talking excessively in his presence.
- Not asking questions when he seems tired.

## فَصْلٌ: فِي تَعْظِيمِ الْعِلْمِ وَأَهْلِهِ

اعْلَمْ بِأَنَّ طَالِبَ الْعِلْمِ لَا يَنَالُ الْعِلْمَ وَلَا يَنْتَفِعُ بِهِ إِلَّا بِتَعْظِيمِ الْعِلْمِ وَأَهْلِهِ، وَتَعْظِيمِ الْأُسْتَاذِ وَتَوْقِيرِهِ.

قِيلَ: مَا وَصَلَ مَنْ وَصَلَ إِلَّا بِالْحُرْمَةِ، وَمَا سَقَطَ مَنْ سَقَطَ إِلَّا بِتَرْكِ الْحُرْمَةِ.

وَقِيلَ: الْحُرْمَةُ خَيْرٌ مِنَ الطَّاعَةِ. أَلَا تَرَىٰ أَنَّ الْإِنْسَانَ لَا يَكْفُرُ بِالْمَعْصِيَةِ، وَإِنَّمَا يَكْفُرُ بِاسْتِخْفَافِهَا، وَبِتَرْكِ الْحُرْمَةِ.

وَمِنْ تَعْظِيمِ الْعِلْمِ تَعْظِيمُ الْأُسْتَاذِ، قَالَ عَلِيٌّ: أَنَا عَبْدُ مَنْ عَلَّمَنِي حَرْفًا وَاحِدًا، إِنْ شَاءَ بَاعَ، وَإِنْ شَاءَ اسْتَرَقَّ، وَإِنْ شَاءَ أَعْتَقَ.

وَقَدْ أُنْشِدْتُ فِي ذَٰلِكَ:

رَأَيْتُ أَحَقَّ الْحَقِّ حَقَّ الْمُعَلِّمِ وَأَوْجَبَهُ حِفْظًا عَلَىٰ كُلِّ مُسْلِمِ
لَقَدْ حَقَّ أَنْ يُهْدَىٰ إِلَيْهِ كَرَامَةً لِتَعْلِيمِ حَرْفٍ وَاحِدٍ أَلْفُ دِرْهَمِ

فَإِنَّ مَنْ عَلَّمَكَ حَرْفًا وَاحِدًا مِمَّا تَحْتَاجُ إِلَيْهِ فِي الدِّينِ فَهُوَ أَبُوكَ فِي الدِّينِ.

وَكَانَ أُسْتَاذُنَا الشَّيْخُ الْإِمَامُ سَدِيدُ الدِّينِ الشِّيرَازِيُّ يَقُولُ: قَالَ مَشَايِخُنَا: مَنْ أَرَادَ أَنْ يَكُونَ ابْنُهُ عَالِمًا يَنْبَغِي أَنْ يُرَاعِيَ الْغُرَبَاءَ مِنَ الْفُقَهَاءِ، وَيُكْرِمَهُمْ وَيُطْعِمَهُمْ وَيُعْطِيَهُمْ شَيْئًا، فَإِنْ لَمْ يَكُنْ ابْنُهُ عَالِمًا يَكُونُ حَفِيدُهُ عَالِمًا.

وَمِنْ تَوْقِيرِ الْمُعَلِّمِ أَلَّا يَمْشِيَ أَمَامَهُ، وَلَا يَجْلِسَ مَكَانَهُ، وَلَا يَبْتَدِئَ

- Being mindful of timing.
- Not knocking on the door, but waiting patiently for the teacher to emerge.

In essence, the student should seek the teacher's pleasure, avoid his displeasure, and follow his instructions – except in matters that would involve disobeying Allah. There is no obedience to the creation if it means disobeying the Creator, as the Prophet ﷺ said: "The worst of people are those whose religion is lost for the worldly gains of others through disobeying the Creator."

الْكَلَامَ عِنْدَهُ إِلَّا بِإِذْنِهِ، وَلَا يُكْثِرُ الْكَلَامَ عِنْدَهُ، وَلَا يَسْأَلَ شَيْئًا عِنْدَ مَلَالَتِهِ وَيُرَاعِيَ الْوَقْتَ، وَلَا يَدُقَّ الْبَابَ؛ بَلْ يَصْبِرَ حَتَّى يَخْرُجَ الْأُسْتَاذُ.

فَالْحَاصِلُ: أَنَّهُ يَطْلُبُ رِضَاهُ، وَيَجْتَنِبُ سُخْطَهُ، وَيَمْتَثِلُ أَمْرَهُ فِي غَيْرِ مَعْصِيَةِ اللَّهِ تَعَالَىٰ؛ فَإِنَّهُ لَا طَاعَةَ لِلْمَخْلُوقِ فِي مَعْصِيَةِ الْخَالِقِ؛ كَمَا قَالَ النَّبِيُّ ﷺ: «إِنَّ شَرَّ النَّاسِ مَنْ يَذْهَبُ دِينُهُ لِدُنْيَا غَيْرِهِ بِمَعْصِيَةِ الْخَالِقِ».

### RESPECTING THE TEACHER ALSO INCLUDES RESPECTING HIS CHILDREN AND THOSE CLOSE TO HIM

Our teacher, Shaykh al-Islām, Burḥān al-Dīn ﵀ – author of *Al-Hidāya* – relayed an anecdote about a notable imam from Bukhara who would stand up if he saw his teacher's son playing in the street, out of respect for his teacher. He was asked about it, to which he replied: "It is the son of my teacher playing with the children in the street. He comes every now and again to the door of the mosque, so when I see him I stand for him our of respect for my teacher."

The Qāḍī al-Imām Fakhr al-Dīn al-Arsābandī was the leader of the imams in Marw, and the Sultan held him in the utmost respect. The Sultan used to say: "I only attained this position through the service of the *ustādh*. Indeed, I used to serve the *ustādh*, the Qāḍī al-Imām Abū Zayd al-Dabbūsī, and I served him and cooked his food [for thirty years] without eating anything from it."

The Shaykh al-Imām al-Ajall Shams al-Aʾimma al-Ḥalwānī ﵀ departed from Bukhara and stayed in a village for a few days due to an incident that befell him. His students visited him, except for the Shaykh al-Imām Shams al-Aʾimma al-Qāḍī Abū Bakr ibn Muhammad al-Zaranjirī (may Allah exalt his rank). When the *shaykh* met him, he said to him: "Why did you not visit me?" He replied: "I was occupied with serving my mother." The *shaykh* said: "You will be granted a long life, but you will not be granted the brilliance of scholarly instruction." And it was so, for he spent most of his time in the villages, and he never established a proper scholarly circle. Whoever causes harm to their *ustādh* is deprived of the blessing of knowledge and derives little benefit from it.

## وَمِنْ تَوْقِيرِهِ: تَوْقِيرُ أَوْلَادِهِ، وَمَنْ يَتَعَلَّقُ بِهِ

وَكَانَ أُسْتَاذُنَا شَيْخُ الْإِسْلَامِ بُرْهَانُ الدِّينِ صَاحِبُ «الهِدَايَةِ» رَحْمَةُ اللَّهِ عَلَيْهِ يَحْكِي: أَنَّ وَاحِدًا مِنْ أَكَابِرِ أَئِمَّةِ بُخَارَىٰ كَانَ يَجْلِسُ مَجْلِسَ الدَّرْسِ، وَكَانَ يَقُومُ فِي خِلَالِ الدَّرْسِ أَحْيَانًا فَسَأَلُوا عَنْهُ، فَقَالَ: إِنَّ ابْنَ أُسْتَاذِي يَلْعَبُ مَعَ الصِّبْيَانِ فِي السِّكَّةِ، وَيَجِيءُ أَحْيَانًا إِلَى بَابِ الْمَسْجِدِ، فَإِذَا رَأَيْتُهُ أَقُومُ لَهُ تَعْظِيمًا لِأُسْتَاذِي.

وَالْقَاضِي الْإِمَامُ فَخْرُ الدِّينِ الْأَرْسَابَنْدِيُّ كَانَ رَئِيسَ الْأَئِمَّةِ فِي مَرْوٍ، وَكَانَ السُّلْطَانُ يَحْتَرِمُهُ غَايَةَ الِاحْتِرَامِ، وَكَانَ يَقُولُ: إِنَّمَا وُجِدْتُ بِهَذَا الْمَنْصِبِ بِخِدْمَةِ الْأُسْتَاذِ، فَإِنِّي كُنْتُ أَخْدُمُ الْأُسْتَاذَ الْقَاضِيَ الْإِمَامَ أَبَا زَيْدٍ الدَّبُوسِيَّ، وَكُنْتُ أَخْدُمُهُ وَأَطْبُخُ طَعَامَهُ [ثَلَاثِينَ سَنَةً] وَلَا آكُلُ مِنْهُ شَيْئًا.

وَكَانَ الشَّيْخُ الْإِمَامُ الْأَجَلُّ شَمْسُ الْأَئِمَّةِ الْحَلْوَانِيُّ رَحِمَةُ اللَّهِ عَلَيْهِ قَدْ خَرَجَ مِنْ بُخَارَىٰ وَسَكَنَ فِي بَعْضِ الْقُرَىٰ أَيَّامًا لِحَادِثَةٍ وَقَعَتْ لَهُ، وَقَدْ زَارَهُ تَلَامِيذُهُ غَيْرَ الشَّيْخِ الْإِمَامِ شَمْسِ الْأَئِمَّةِ الْقَاضِي أَبِي بَكْرِ بْنِ مُحَمَّدٍ الزَّرَنْجَرِيُّ رَحِمَهُ اللَّهُ تَعَالَىٰ فَقَالَ لَهُ حِينَ لَقِيَهُ: لِمَاذَا لَمْ تَزُرْنِي؟ قَالَ: كُنْتُ مَشْغُولًا بِخِدْمَةِ الْوَالِدَةِ. قَالَ: تُرْزَقُ الْعُمْرَ، وَلَا تُرْزَقُ رَوْنَقَ الدَّرْسِ. وَكَانَ كَذَلِكَ، فَإِنَّهُ كَانَ يَسْكُنُ فِي أَكْثَرِ أَوْقَاتِهِ فِي الْقُرَىٰ، وَلَمْ يَنْتَظِمْ لَهُ الدَّرْسُ فَمَنْ تَأَذَّىٰ مِنْهُ أُسْتَاذُهُ يُحْرَمُ بَرَكَةَ

*Indeed, the teacher and the doctor will not offer sincere advice if they are not honoured.*
*Be patient with your ailment if you've been harsh to the doctor;*
*Be content with your ignorance if you've been harsh to the teacher.*

A story is related about Ḥārūn al-Rashīd sending his son to al-Asmāʿī to teach him knowledge and manners. One day, he (Ḥārūn al-Rashīd) saw him (al-Asmāʿī) performing ablution and washing his foot, while the caliph's [own] son was pouring water over his [the teacher's] foot. He reproached al-Aṣmaʿī, saying: "I sent him to you to teach and discipline him. Why did you not instruct him to pour water with one hand and wash your foot with the other?"

Part of honouring knowledge is honouring books. A student should not take a book except in a state of ritual purity. One scholar claimed he only attained knowledge through reverence, never touching paper except when purified.

It is narrated that Shaykh Shams al-Aʾimma al-Ḥalwānī ﵀ said: "I attained this knowledge through reverence, for I never took the paper except in a state of purity."

Shaykh al-Imām Shams al-Aʾimma al-Sarakhasī suffered from abdominal illness one night and was engaged in repetition [of knowledge]. He performed ablution seventeen times that night because he would not engage in repetition except in a state of purity. This is because knowledge is light, and ablution is light; thus, the light of knowledge increases with it.

Among the obligatory acts of reverence is not to extend one's legs towards the book, to place books of *tafsīr* above other books [out of respect], and not to place anything else upon the book.

Our master, the eminent *shaykh*, Imām Burhān al-Dīn ﵀ used to narrate about a *shaykh*: "A jurist had placed an inkwell on a book, and he said to him in Persian: 'Do not do this.'"

Our master, the eminent imam and judge, known as Qāḍī

الْعِلْمِ وَلَا يَنْتَفِعُ بِالْعِلْمِ إِلَّا قَلِيلًا.

إِنَّ الْمُعَلِّمَ وَالطَّبِيبَ كِلَاهُمَا لَا يَنْصَحَانِ إِذَا هُمَا لَمْ يُكْرَمَا

فَاصْبِرْ لِدَائِكَ إِنْ جَفَوْتَ طَبِيبَهُ وَاقْنَعْ بِجَهْلِكَ إِنْ جَفَوْتَ مُعَلِّمَا

وَحُكِيَ أَنَّ الْخَلِيفَةَ هَارُونَ الرَّشِيدُ بَعَثَ ابْنَهُ إِلَى الْأَصْمَعِيِّ لِيُعَلِّمَهُ الْعِلْمَ وَالْأَدَبَ، فَرَآهُ يَوْمًا يَتَوَضَّأُ وَيَغْسِلُ رِجْلَهُ، وَابْنُ الْخَلِيفَةِ يَصُبُّ الْمَاءَ عَلَى رِجْلِهِ، فَعَاتَبَ الْأَصْمَعِيَّ فِي ذَلِكَ بِقَوْلِهِ: إِنَّمَا بَعَثْتُهُ إِلَيْكَ لِتُعَلِّمَهُ وَتُؤَدِّبَهُ، فَلِمَاذَا لَمْ تَأْمُرْهُ بِأَنْ يَصُبَّ الْمَاءَ بِإِحْدَى يَدَيْهِ، وَيَغْسِلَ بِالْأُخْرَى رِجْلَكَ؟ **وَمِنْ تَعْظِيمِ الْعِلْمِ**: تَعْظِيمُ الْكِتَابِ، فَيَنْبَغِي لِطَالِبِ الْعِلْمِ أَلَّا يَأْخُذَ الْكِتَابَ إِلَّا بِطَهَارَةٍ. **وَحُكِيَ** عَنِ الشَّيْخِ شَمْسِ الْأَئِمَّةِ الْحَلْوَانِيِّ رَحْمَةُ اللهِ عَلَيْهِ أَنَّهُ قَالَ: إِنَّمَا نِلْتُ هَذَا الْعِلْمَ بِالتَّعْظِيمِ، فَإِنِّي مَا أَخَذْتُ الْكَاغَدَ إِلَّا بِطَهَارَةٍ. **وَالشَّيْخُ** الْإِمَامُ شَمْسُ الْأَئِمَّةِ السَّرَخْسِيُّ كَانَ مَبْطُونًا فِي لَيْلَةٍ، وَكَانَ يُكَرِّرُ، وَتَوَضَّأَ فِي تِلْكَ اللَّيْلَةِ سَبْعَ عَشَرَةَ مَرَّةً لِأَنَّهُ كَانَ لَا يُكَرِّرُ إِلَّا بِالطَّهَارَةِ؛ وَهَذَا لِأَنَّ الْعِلْمَ نُورٌ وَالْوُضُوءَ نُورٌ، فَيَزْدَادُ نُورُ الْعِلْمِ بِهِ. **وَمِنَ** التَّعْظِيمِ الْوَاجِبِ أَلَّا يَمُدَّ الرِّجْلَ إِلَى الْكِتَابِ، وَيَضَعَ كُتُبَ التَّفْسِيرِ فَوْقَ سَائِرِ الْكُتُبِ [تَعْظِيمًا]، وَلَا يَضَعُ شَيْئًا آخَرَ عَلَى الْكِتَابِ. **وَكَانَ أُسْتَاذُنَا** الشَّيْخُ الْإِمَامُ بُرْهَانُ الدِّينِ رَحِمَهُ اللهُ تَعَالَى يَحْكِي عَنْ شَيْخٍ مِنَ الْمَشَايِخِ: أَنَّ فَقِيهًا كَانَ وَضَعَ الْمِحْبَرَةَ عَلَى الْكِتَابِ، فَقَالَ لَهُ [بِالْفَارِسِيَّةِ]: بَرْ نَيَا بِي. وَكَانَ أُسْتَاذُنَا الْقَاضِي الْإِمَامُ الْأَجَلُّ فَخْرُ

Khān ﵀ would say: "If he did not intend disrespect, there is no harm in this, but it is preferable to avoid it."

Among the ways of honouring [knowledge] is to improve the writing of a book and not to write carelessly, leaving margins except out of necessity.

Abū Ḥanīfah ﵀ saw a scribe writing carelessly and said: "Do not write sloppily. If you live, you will regret it, and if you die, you will be cursed." By this, he meant that when you grow old and your eyesight weakens, you will regret it.

It is narrated about Shaykh Imām Majd al-Dīn al-Sarakhasī that he said: "Whatever we wrote carelessly, we regretted; whatever we selected, we regretted; whatever we did not compare, we regretted."

It is appropriate that the page division be square, for this is the method of Abū Ḥanīfah ﵀ and it is easier for lifting, placing, and studying. It is appropriate that there be no red in the book, for this is the practice of philosophers, not of the predecessors. Many of our *shaykhs* disliked using red ink.

Part of honouring knowledge is honouring one's companions in seeking knowledge and learning, and those from whom one learns. Flattery is condemned except in seeking knowledge.

It is appropriate for the student to flatter his teacher and companions to benefit from them.

The student should listen to knowledge and wisdom with reverence and respect, even if hearing a single matter or wisdom a thousand times. It is said: "Whoever does not honour a piece of knowledge after hearing it a thousand times with the same reverence as the first time is unworthy of that knowledge."

It is appropriate for the student not to choose the category of knowledge by himself but to defer to the teacher, for the teacher has gained experience in this and knows best what is appropriate for each person and what suits their nature.

The Shaykh Imām, the most eminent teacher, Burḥān al-Haqq wa al-Dīn ﵀ would say: "In earlier times, students

الدِّينِ الْمَعْرُوف بِقَاضِي خَانْ رَحِمَهُ اللهُ تَعَالَىٰ يَقُولُ: إِنْ لَمْ يُرِدْ بِذَلِكَ الاسْتِخْفَافَ فَلَا بَأْسَ بِذَلِكَ، وَالْأَوْلَىٰ أَنْ يَحْتَرِزَ عَنْهُ.

وَمِنَ التَّعْظِيمِ: أَنْ يُجَوِّدَ كِتَابَةَ الْكِتَابِ، وَلَا يُقَرْمِطَ وَيَتْرُكَ الْحَاشِيَةَ إِلَّا عِنْدَ الضَّرُورَةِ. وَرَأَى أَبُو حَنِيفَةَ رَحِمَهُ اللهُ تَعَالَىٰ كَاتِبًا يُقَرْمِطُ فِي الْكِتَابَةِ فَقَالَ: «لَا تُقَرْمِطْ خَطَّكَ، إِنْ عِشْتَ تَنْدَمْ، وَإِنْ مِتَّ تُشْتَمْ»؛ يَعْنِي إِذَا شِخْتَ وَضَعُفَ نُورُ بَصَرِكَ نَدِمْتَ عَلَىٰ ذَلِكَ.

وَحُكِيَ عَنِ الشَّيْخِ الْإِمَامِ مَجْدِ الدِّينِ الصَّرْخَكِيِّ؛ حُكِيَ أَنَّهُ قَالَ: مَا قَرْمَطْنَا نَدِمْنَا، وَمَا انْتَخَبْنَا نَدِمْنَا، وَمَا لَمْ نُقَابِلْ نَدِمْنَا. **وَيَنْبَغِي** أَنْ يَكُونَ تَقْطِيعُ الْكِتَابِ مُرَبَّعًا، فَإِنَّهُ تَقْطِيعُ أَبِي حَنِيفَةَ رَحِمَهُ اللهُ تَعَالَىٰ وَهُوَ أَيْسَرُ عَلَى الرَّفْعِ وَالْوَضْعِ وَالْمُطَالَعَةِ.

وَيَنْبَغِي أَلَّا يَكُونَ فِي الْكِتَابِ شَيْءٌ مِنَ الْحُمْرَةِ، فَإِنَّهُ مِنْ صَنِيعِ الْفَلَاسِفَةِ لَا صَنِيعِ السَّلَفِ، وَمِنْ مَشَايِخِنَا كَرِهُوا اسْتِعْمَالَ الْمُرَكَّبِ الْأَحْمَرِ. **وَمِنْ** تَعْظِيمِ الْعِلْمِ: تَعْظِيمُ الشُّرَكَاءِ فِي طَلَبِ الْعِلْمِ وَالدَّرْسِ وَمَنْ يُتَعَلَّمُ مِنْهُ، وَالتَّمَلُّقُ مَذْمُومٌ إِلَّا فِي طَلَبِ الْعِلْمِ. فَإِنَّهُ يَنْبَغِي أَنْ يَتَمَلَّقَ لِأُسْتَاذِهِ وَشُرَكَائِهِ لِيَسْتَفِيدَ مِنْهُمْ. **وَيَنْبَغِي** لِطَالِبِ الْعِلْمِ أَنْ يَسْتَمِعَ الْعِلْمَ وَالْحِكْمَةَ بِالتَّعْظِيمِ وَالْحُرْمَةِ، وَإِنْ سَمِعَ مَسْأَلَةً وَاحِدَةً أَوْ حِكْمَةً وَاحِدَةً أَلْفَ مَرَّةٍ. قِيلَ: مَنْ لَمْ يَكُنْ تَعْظِيمُهُ بَعْدَ أَلْفِ مَرَّةٍ كَتَعْظِيمِهِ فِي أَوَّلِ مَرَّةٍ فَلَيْسَ بِأَهْلٍ لِلْعِلْمِ.

وَيَنْبَغِي لِطَالِبِ الْعِلْمِ أَلَّا يَخْتَارَ نَوْعَ الْعِلْمِ بِنَفْسِهِ، بَلْ يُفَوِّضُ أَمْرَهُ إِلَى الْأُسْتَاذِ، فَإِنَّ الْأُسْتَاذَ قَدْ حَصَلَ لَهُ التَّجَارِبُ فِي ذَلِكَ، فَكَانَ

would defer their learning to their teachers and would reach their goals and desires. Now they choose for themselves, so they do not attain their purpose in knowledge and jurisprudence."

It is narrated that Muhammad ibn Ismā'īl al-Bukhārī ﵀ began with a book on prayer with Muhammad ibn al-Ḥasan ﵀ who said to him: "Go and learn Hadith", seeing that this knowledge was more suited to his nature. So he sought Hadith knowledge and became preeminent among all Hadith scholars.

The student should not sit close to the teacher without necessity, but there should be a bow's length between them, as this is closer to showing respect.

The student should be cautious of blameworthy character traits, for they are like spiritual dogs. The Prophet ﷺ said: "Angels do not enter a house with a dog or an image", and a person learns through an angel.

Blameworthy character traits are known in *The Book of Character*, and our book cannot bear their explanation, especially regarding arrogance. With arrogance, knowledge is not attained.

It is said: "Knowledge is war for the one who is haughty like a flood is war for the high ground."[5]

---

(5) Translator: Just as water in a flood cannot settle on high ground and instead flows away, knowledge cannot reside or take root in someone who is haughty or arrogant. Knowledge requires humility, openness, and a readiness to learn, while arrogance creates a barrier that prevents the acceptance or internalisation of wisdom.

أَعْرَفَ بِمَا يَنْبَغِي لِكُلِّ أَحَدٍ وَمَا يَلِيقُ بِطَبِيعَتِهِ. **وَكَانَ** الشَّيْخُ الْإِمَامُ الْأَجَلُّ الْأُسْتَاذُ بُرْهَانُ الْحَقِّ وَالدِّينِ رَحِمَهُ اللَّهُ تَعَالَىٰ يَقُولُ: كَانَ طَلَبَةُ الْعِلْمِ فِي الزَّمَانِ الْأَوَّلِ يُفَوِّضُونَ أَمْرَهُمْ فِي التَّعَلُّمِ إِلَىٰ أُسْتَاذِهِمْ، وَكَانُوا يَصِلُونَ إِلَىٰ مَقْصُودِهِمْ وَمُرَادِهِمْ، وَالْآنَ يَخْتَارُونَ بِأَنْفُسِهِمْ، فَلَا يَحْصُلُ مَقْصُودُهُمْ مِنَ الْعِلْمِ وَالْفِقْهِ. **وَكَانَ** يُحْكَىٰ أَنَّ مُحَمَّدَ بْنَ إِسْمَاعِيلَ الْبُخَارِيَّ رَحِمَهُ اللَّهُ تَعَالَىٰ كَانَ بَدَأَ بِكِتَابِ الصَّلَاةِ عَلَىٰ مُحَمَّدِ بْنِ الْحَسَنِ رَحِمَهُ اللَّهُ تَعَالَىٰ، فَقَالَ لَهُ مُحَمَّدُ بْنُ الْحَسَنِ: اذْهَبْ وَتَعَلَّمْ عِلْمَ الْحَدِيثِ، لِمَا رَأَىٰ أَنَّ ذَلِكَ الْعِلْمَ أَلْيَقُ بِطَبْعِهِ، فَطَلَبَ عِلْمَ الْحَدِيثِ، فَصَارَ فِيهِ مُقَدَّمًا عَلَىٰ جَمِيعِ أَئِمَّةِ الْحَدِيثِ.

وَيَنْبَغِي لِطَالِبِ الْعِلْمِ أَنْ لَا يَجْلِسَ قَرِيبًا مِنَ الْأُسْتَاذِ عِنْدَ السَّبَقِ بِغَيْرِ ضَرُورَةٍ؛ بَلْ يَنْبَغِي أَنْ يَكُونَ بَيْنَهُ وَبَيْنَ الْأُسْتَاذِ قَدْرَ الْقَوْسِ، فَإِنَّهُ أَقْرَبُ إِلَى التَّعْظِيمِ.

وَيَنْبَغِي لِطَالِبِ الْعِلْمِ أَنْ يَحْتَرِزَ عَنِ الْأَخْلَاقِ الذَّمِيمَةِ، فَإِنَّهَا كِلَابٌ مَعْنَوِيَّةٌ، وَقَدْ قَالَ رَسُولُ اللَّهِ ﷺ: «لَا تَدْخُلُ الْمَلَائِكَةُ بَيْتًا فِيهِ كَلْبٌ أَوْ صُورَةٌ»، وَإِنَّمَا يَتَعَلَّمُ الْإِنْسَانُ بِوَاسِطَةِ مَلَكٍ. **وَالْأَخْلَاقُ** الذَّمِيمَةُ تُعْرَفُ فِي «كِتَابِ الْأَخْلَاقِ» وَكِتَابُنَا هَذَا لَا يَحْتَمِلُ بَيَانَهَا، خُصُوصًا عَنِ التَّكَبُّرِ وَمَعَ التَّكَبُّرِ لَا يَحْصُلُ الْعِلْمُ. قِيلَ:

الْعِلْمُ حَرْبٌ [لِلْفَتَى] الْمُتَعَالِي     كَالسَّيْلِ حَرْبٌ لِلْمَكَانِ الْعَالِي

Then, there is no escape for a student of knowledge from being serious, persistent, and committed. This is alluded to in the Qur'an by His saying: "O Yahyā, take the Book with strength" [*Maryam,* 12] and "Those who strive in Our cause, We will surely guide them to Our paths" [*Al-'Ankabūt,* 69].

It was said:

*By effort, not by fortune, is every glory attained,*
*Can mere fortune, without effort, lead to glory?*
*How many a servant takes the place of a free man,*
*And how many a free man takes the place of a servant?*

It was said: "Whoever seeks something with seriousness will find it, and whoever knocks at the door persistently will enter."

It was said: "In proportion to your patience, you will attain what you desire."

It was said: "In learning and understanding, three are needed: the student, the teacher, and the father if he is still alive."

The Shaykh al-Imām, the most venerable teacher, Sadīd al-Dīn al-Shirāzī recited for al-Shāfi'ī ﷺ:

*Effort brings near every distant matter,*
*And effort unlocks every closed door.*
*The most deserving of Allah's creation to worry*
*Is one with ambition, yet burdened by a constrained life.*
*A sign of divine decree and judgment*
*Is the misery of the wise and the comfort of the fool.*
*But one who is gifted with intellect is often denied wealth;*
*Two opposites, separated by the greatest divide.*

And it was recited for another:

*You wish to become a jurist and debater*
*Without effort, but madness takes many forms.*
*If wealth cannot be attained without hardship,*

## فَصلٌ فِي الجِدِّ وَالْمُوَاظَبَةِ وَالهِمَّةِ

ثُمَّ لا بُدَّ مِنَ الجِدِّ وَالْمُوَاظَبَةِ وَالْمُلازَمَةِ لِطَالِبِ الْعِلْمِ، وَإِلَيْهِ الْإِشَارَةُ فِي الْقُرْآنِ بِقَوْلِهِ تَعَالَىٰ: ﴿يَا يَحْيَىٰ خُذِ الْكِتَابَ بِقُوَّةٍ﴾ [مريم: ١٢]، وَقَوْلِهِ تَعَالَىٰ: ﴿وَالَّذِينَ جَاهَدُوا فِينَا لَنَهْدِيَنَّهُمْ سُبُلَنَا﴾ [العنكبوت: ٦٩]. قِيلَ:

بِجِدٍّ لَا بِجَدٍّ كُلُّ مَجْدٍ　　فَهَلْ جَدٌّ بِلَا جِدٍّ بِمَجْدِ
فَكَمْ عَبْدٍ يَقُومُ مَقَامَ حُرٍّ　　وَكَمْ حُرٍّ يَقُومُ مَقَامَ عَبْدِ

وَقِيلَ: مَنْ طَلَبَ شَيْئًا وَجَدَّ وَجَدَ، وَمَنْ قَرَعَ الْبَابَ وَلَجَّ وَلَجَ.

وَقِيلَ: بِقَدْرِ مَا تَتَعَنَّىٰ تَنَالُ مَا تَتَمَنَّىٰ.

وَقِيلَ: يُحْتَاجُ فِي التَّعَلُّمِ وَالتَّفَقُّهِ إِلَىٰ جِدِّ ثَلاثَةٍ: الْمُتَعَلِّمِ، وَالْأُسْتَاذِ، وَالْأَبِ إِنْ كَانَ فِي الْأَحْيَاءِ.

أَنْشَدَنِي الشَّيْخُ الْإِمَامُ الْأَجَلُّ الْأُسْتَاذُ سَدِيدُ الدِّينِ الشِّيرَازِيُّ لِلشَّافِعِيِّ رَحِمَهُمَا اللَّهُ:

الجِدُّ يُدْنِي كُلَّ أَمْرٍ شَاسِعٍ　　وَالجِدُّ يَفْتَحُ كُلَّ بَابٍ مُغْلَقِ
وَأَحَقُّ خَلْقِ اللهِ بِالْهَمِّ امْرُؤٌ　　ذُو هِمَّةٍ يُبْلَى بِعَيْشٍ ضَيِّقِ
وَمِنَ الدَّلِيلِ عَلَى الْقَضَاءِ وَحُكْمِهِ　　بُؤْسُ اللَّبِيبِ وَطِيبُ عَيْشِ الْأَحْمَقِ
لَكِنْ مَنْ رُزِقَ الحِجَا حُرِمَ الْغِنَى　　ضِدَّانِ يَفْتَرِقَانِ أَيَّ تَفَرُّقِ

وَأُنْشِدْتُ لِغَيْرِهِ:

تَمَنَّيْتَ أَنْ تُمْسِي فَقِيهًا مُنَاظِرًا　　بِغَيْرِ عَنَاءٍ وَالجُنُونُ فُنُونُ

*Then how can knowledge be gained without toil?*

Abū al-Ṭayyib al-Mutanabbī said:

*I have not seen among the faults of people a flaw*
*Like the failure of those capable of perfection.*

And a student of knowledge must not miss the nights of wakefulness, as the poet said:

*By the measure of toil, greatness is attained,*
*And whoever seeks loftiness stays awake through the nights.*
*You aspire to honour, yet you sleep at night;*
*It is only the diver who retrieves the pearls.*
*Excellence is achieved through lofty aspirations,*
*And a person's honour lies in sleepless nights.*
*I forsook sleep at night, my Lord,*
*For Your pleasure, O Master of all masters.*
*Whoever seeks greatness without effort*
*Wastes their life in pursuit of the impossible.*
*So guide me to attain knowledge,*
*And grant me the highest ranks of greatness.*

It was said: "Make the night your mount, and you will reach your hopes."

The author said: "And I happened to compose in this meaning:

*Whoever wishes to encompass their aspirations entirely,*
*Let them make their nights a vessel for pursuing them.*
*Reduce your food so you may gain wakefulness,*
*If, my friend, you wish to attain perfection."*

It was said: "Whoever stays awake at night has gladdened his heart during the day."

A student of knowledge must persist in studying and repeating lessons in the first and last parts of the night, for the time

وَلَيْسَ اكْتِسَابُ الْمَالِ دُونَ مَشَقَّةٍ تَحَمُّلُهَا فَالْعِلْمُ كَيْفَ يَكُونُ؟

قَالَ أَبُو الطَّيِّبِ الْمُتَنَبِّي:

وَلَمْ أَرَ فِي عُيُوبِ النَّاسِ عَيْبًا كَنَقْصِ الْقَادِرِينَ عَلَى التَّمَامِ

وَلَا بُدَّ لِطَالِبِ الْعِلْمِ مِنْ سَهَرِ اللَّيَالِي كَمَا قَالَ الشَّاعِرُ:

بِقَدْرِ الْكَدِّ تُكْتَسَبُ الْمَعَالِي وَمَنْ طَلَبَ الْعُلَى سَهِرَ اللَّيَالِي
تَرُومُ الْعِزَّ ثُمَّ تَنَامُ لَيْلًا يَغُوصُ الْبَحْرَ مَنْ طَلَبَ اللَّآلِي
عُلُوُّ الكَعْبِ بِالْهِمَمِ الْعَوَالِي وَعِزُّ الْمَرْءِ فِي سَهَرِ اللَّيَالِي
تَرَكْتُ النَّومَ رَبِّي فِي اللَّيَالِي لِأَجْلِ رِضَاكَ يَا مَوْلَى الْمَوَالِي
وَمَنْ رَامَ الْعُلَى مِنْ غَيْرِ كَدٍّ أَضَاعَ الْعُمْرَ فِي طَلَبِ الْمُحَالِ
فَوَفِّقْنِي إِلَى تَحْصِيلِ عِلْمٍ وَبَلِّغْنِي إِلَى أَقْصَى الْمَعَالِي

قِيلَ: اتَّخِذِ اللَّيْلَ جَمَلًا، تُدْرِكْ بِهِ أَمَلًا.

قَالَ الْمُصَنِّفُ: وَقَدِ اتَّفَقَ لِي نَظْمٌ فِي هَذَا الْمَعْنَى:

مَنْ شَاءَ أَنْ يَحْتَوِي آمَالَهُ جُمَلًا فَلْيَتَّخِذْ لَيْلَهُ فِي دَرْكِهَا جَمَلَا
أَقْلِلْ طَعَامَكَ كَيْ تَحْظَى بِهِ سَهَرًا إِنْ شِئْتَ يَا صَاحِبِي أَنْ تَبْلُغَ الْكَمَلَا

وَقِيلَ: مَنْ أَسْهَرَ نَفْسَهُ بِاللَّيْلِ، فَقَدْ فَرَّحَ قَلْبَهُ بِالنَّهَارِ.

وَلَا بُدَّ لِطَالِبِ الْعِلْمِ مِنَ الْمُوَاظَبَةِ عَلَى الدَّرْسِ وَالتَّكْرَارِ فِي أَوَّلِ اللَّيْلِ وَآخِرِهِ؛ فَإِنَّ مَا بَيْنَ الْعِشَاءَيْنِ، وَوَقْتَ السَّحَرِ، وَقْتٌ مُبَارَكٌ.

between the two night prayers and at dawn is a blessed time.[6]

It was said in this meaning:

*O seeker of knowledge, embrace piety,*
*Avoid excessive sleep, and abandon satiety.*
*Persevere in studying and never part from it,*
*For knowledge thrives and rises through diligence in study.*

So seize the days of youth and its vigour, as it was said:

*In proportion to your effort, you achieve what you desire;*
*Whoever seeks lofty aspirations must rise in the night.*
*Seize the days of youth and make the most of them,*
*For youth, indeed, does not endure forever.*

And one should not exhaust oneself to the point of weakness that prevents work, but rather use gentleness in this – and gentleness is a great principle in all things.

The Prophet ﷺ said: "Indeed, this religion is profound, so approach it with gentleness. Do not make yourself resentful of worshipping Allah, the Exalted, for the one who is overly zealous neither traverses the land nor preserves his mount."

He ﷺ also said: "Your self is your mount, so be gentle with it."

A student of knowledge must have a high ambition in knowledge, for a person flies with his ambition like a bird flies with its wings.

Abū al-Ṭayyib ؒ said:

*The magnitude of resolve matches the people of determination,*
*And noble deeds come in proportion to the noble.*
*What is small appears great in the eyes of the small,*
*And what is great appears small in the eyes of the great.*

(6) Translator: It is a blessed time for many reasons, one of which is its unique sense of expansiveness – an opportunity to accomplish far more than what is typically achievable at other times.

قِيلَ فِي هَذَا الْمَعْنَىٰ:

يَا طَالِبَ الْعِلْمِ بَاشِرِ الْوَرَعَا ... وَجَانِبِ النَّوْمَ وَاتْرُكِ الشِّبَعَا
وَدَاوِمْ عَلَى الدَّرْسِ لَا تُفَارِقْهُ ... فَإِنَّ الْعِلْمَ بِالدَّرْسِ قَامَ وَارْتَفَعَا

فَيَغْتَنِمُ أَيَّامَ الْحَدَاثَةِ وَعُنْفُوَانَ الشَّبَابِ، كَمَا قِيلَ:

بِقَدْرِ الكَدِّ تُعْطَىٰ مَا تَرُومُ ... فَمَنْ رَامَ الْمُنَىٰ لَيْلًا يَقُومُ
وَأَيَّامَ الْحَدَاثَةِ فَاغْتَنِمْهَا ... أَلَا إِنَّ الْحَدَاثَةَ لَا تَدُومُ

وَلَا يُجْهِدُ نَفْسَهُ جَهْدًا يُضْعِفُ النَّفْسَ حَتَّى يَنْقَطِعَ عَنِ الْعَمَلِ؛ بَلْ يَسْتَعْمِلُ الرِّفْقَ فِي ذَلِكَ، وَالرِّفْقُ أَصْلٌ عَظِيمٌ فِي جَمِيعِ الْأَشْيَاءِ.

قَالَ رَسُولُ اللَّهِ ﷺ: «أَلَا إِنَّ هَذَا الدِّينَ مَتِينٌ، فَأَوْغِلْ فِيهِ بِرِفْقٍ، وَلَا تُبَغِّضْ نَفْسَكَ فِي عِبَادَةِ اللَّهِ تَعَالَىٰ فَإِنَّ الْمُنْبَتَّ لَا أَرْضًا قَطَعَ، وَلَا ظَهْرًا أَبْقَىٰ».

وَقَالَ عَلَيْهِ السَّلَامُ: نَفْسُكَ مَطِيَّتُكَ فَارْفُقْ بِهَا».

فَلَا بُدَّ لِطَالِبِ الْعِلْمِ مِنَ الْهِمَّةِ الْعَالِيَةِ فِي الْعِلْمِ، فَإِنَّ الْمَرْءَ يَطِيرُ بِهِمَّتِهِ كَالطَّيْرِ يَطِيرُ بِجَنَاحَيْهِ.

وَقَالَ أَبُو الطَّيِّبِ رَحِمَهُ اللهُ:

عَلَىٰ قَدْرِ أَهْلِ الْعَزْمِ تَأْتِي الْعَزَائِمُ ... وَتَأْتِي عَلَىٰ قَدْرِ الْكِرَامِ الْمَكَارِمُ
وَتَعْظُمُ فِي عَيْنِ الصَّغِيرِ صِغَارُهَا ... وَتَصْغُرُ فِي عَيْنِ الْعَظِيمِ الْعَظَائِمُ

وَالرُّكْنُ فِي تَحْصِيلِ الْأَشْيَاءِ الْجِدُّ وَالْهِمَّةُ الْعَالِيَةُ، فَمَنْ كَانَتْ هِمَّتُهُ حِفْظَ جَمِيعِ كُتُبِ مُحَمَّدِ بْنِ الْحَسَنِ، وَاقْتَرَنَ بِذَلِكَ الْجِدُّ وَالْمُوَاظَبَةُ،

The cornerstone of achieving goals is diligence and lofty aspiration. If someone's aspiration is to memorise all the books of Muhammad ibn al-Ḥasan, and this is accompanied by diligence and consistency, it is likely that he will memorise most of them or at least half. However, if he possesses lofty aspirations without diligence, or diligence without lofty aspirations, he will attain only a little knowledge.

The esteemed Shaykh Imām Radīy al-Dīn al-Naysābūrī mentioned in his book *Makārim al-Akhlāq* that when Dhū al-Qarnayn intended to travel and take control of the East and West, he consulted the wise and said: "How can I embark on such a journey with the dominion I already possess? Surely, this world is fleeting and insignificant, and worldly dominion is a trivial matter. Would this not contradict the spirit of lofty ambition?" The wise responded: "Travel so that you may attain dominion over both this world and the Hereafter." He replied: "This is indeed better."

The Messenger of Allah ﷺ said: "Indeed, Allah loves lofty matters and despises trivial ones."

It is also said:

*Do not rush your affairs; persevere in them,*
*For nothing aids success like persistence.*

It was reported that Abū Ḥanīfah ﷺ said to Abū Yūsuf: "You were slow-witted, but perseverance elevated you. Beware of laziness, for it is a curse and a grave affliction."

Shaykh Imām Abū Naṣr al-Ṣaffār al-Anṣārī said:

*O soul, O soul, do not slacken in deeds,*
*In righteousness, justice, and kindness whilst there is time,*
*For those who engage in good deeds rejoice,*
*Whilst laziness brings affliction and regret.*

The author said: "I reflected on this and composed the following:

فَالظَّاهِرُ أَنَّهُ يَحْفَظُ أَكْثَرَهَا أَوْ نِصْفَهَا، فَأَمَّا إِذَا كَانَتْ لَهُ هِمَّةٌ عَالِيَةٌ وَلَمْ يَكُنْ لَهُ جِدٌّ، أَوْ كَانَ لَهُ جِدٌّ وَلَمْ تَكُنْ لَهُ هِمَّةٌ عَالِيَةٌ لَا يَحْصُلُ لَهُ الْعِلْمُ إِلَّا قَلِيلًا.

وَذَكَرَ الشَّيْخُ الْإِمَامُ الْأَجَلُّ الْأُسْتَاذُ رَضِيُّ الدِّينِ النَّيْسَابُورِيُّ فِي كِتَابِ «مَكَارِمِ الْأَخْلَاقِ»: أَنَّ ذَا الْقَرْنَيْنِ لَمَّا أَرَادَ أَنْ يُسَافِرَ لِيَسْتَوْلِيَ عَلَى الْمَشْرِقِ وَالْمَغْرِبِ، شَاوَرَ الْحُكَمَاءَ وَقَالَ: كَيْفَ أُسَافِرُ بِهَذَا الْقَدْرِ مِنَ الْمُلْكِ، فَإِنَّ الدُّنْيَا قَلِيلَةٌ فَانِيَةٌ، وَمُلْكُ الدُّنْيَا أَمْرٌ حَقِيرٌ، فَلَيْسَ هَذَا مِنْ عُلُوِّ الهِمَّةِ؟ فَقَالَ الْحُكَمَاءُ: سَافِرْ لِيَحْصُلَ لَكَ مُلْكُ الدُّنْيَا وَالْآخِرَةِ، فَقَالَ: هَذَا أَحْسَنُ.

وَقَالَ رَسُولُ اللَّهِ ﷺ: «إِنَّ اللَّهَ يُحِبُّ مَعَالِيَ الْأُمُورِ وَيَكْرَهُ سَفْسَافَهَا».

وَقِيلَ:

فَلَا تَعْجَلْ بِأَمْرِكَ وَاسْتَدِمْهُ ... فَمَا صَلَّى عَصَاكَ كَمُسْتَدِيمٍ

قِيلَ: قَالَ أَبُو حَنِيفَةَ رَحِمَهُ اللهُ لِأَبِي يُوسُفَ: كُنْتَ بَلِيدًا أَخْرَجَتْكَ الْمُوَاظَبَةُ، وَإِيَّاكَ وَالْكَسَلَ فَإِنَّهُ شُؤْمٌ وَآفَةٌ عَظِيمَةٌ.

قَالَ الشَّيْخُ الْإِمَامُ أَبُو نَصْرٍ الصَّفَّارِ الْأَنْصَارِيُّ:

يَا نَفْسِ يَا نَفْسِ لَا تُرْخِي عَنِ الْعَمَلِ ... فِي الْبِرِّ وَالْعَدْلِ وَالْإِحْسَانِ فِي مَهَلِ
فَكُلُّ ذِي عَمَلٍ فِي الْخَيْرِ مُغْتَبِطٌ ... وَفِي بَلَاءٍ وَشُؤْمٍ كُلُّ ذِي كَسَلِ

قَالَ الْمُصَنِّفُ: وَقَدِ اتَّفَقَ لِي فِي هَذَا الْمَعْنَى:

*O my soul, abandon laziness and procrastination,*
*Or resign yourself to humiliation,*
*For the lazy attain nothing but regret*
*And deprivation of their aspirations."*

It is also said:

*How many shames, incapacities, and regrets*
*Are born of a person's laziness?*
*Beware of laziness when seeking answers to doubts.*
*What you know and what escapes you, enquire about them.*

It is also said: "Laziness stems from a lack of contemplation on the virtues of knowledge. One must exhaust oneself in pursuit, diligence, and perseverance, reflecting on the benefits of knowledge, for knowledge endures [with the preservation of information], while wealth perishes."

As Amīr al-Mu'minīn 'Alī ibn Abī Ṭālib (may Allah honour his face) said:

*We are content with the Almighty's division among us:*
*To us, knowledge; to our enemies, wealth.*
*For wealth perishes swiftly,*
*But knowledge remains, unceasing and eternal.*

Beneficial knowledge earns a person good remembrance and endures beyond death. It is an everlasting life. Shaykh Imām Ẓahīr al-Dīn, mufti of the imams, Ḥasan ibn 'Alī, known as al-Marghīnānī, recited: "The ignorant are dead even before their death, / Whilst the learned, even if they die, remain alive."

Shaykh Imām Burhān al-Dīn ﵀ recited:

*Ignorance is a death for its people before their demise,*
*Their bodies are graves even before they are buried.*
*And if a person does not live through knowledge, they are dead,*
*For at resurrection, they will have no revival.*

Another said:

دَعِي نَفْسِي التَّكَاسُلَ وَالتَّوَانِي      وَإِلَّا فَاثْبُتِي فِي ذَا الْهَوَانِ
فَلَمْ أَرَ لِلْكُسَالَى الْحَظَّ تُحْظَى      سِوَى نَدَمٍ وَحِرْمَانِ الْأَمَانِي

وَقِيلَ:

كَمْ مِنْ حَيَاءٍ وَكَمْ عَجْزٍ وَكَمْ نَدَمٍ      جَمٍّ تَوَلَّدَ لِلْإِنْسَانِ مِنْ كَسَلِ
إِيَّاكَ عَنْ كَسَلٍ فِي الْبَحْثِ عَنْ شُبَهٍ      فَمَا عَلِمْتَ وَمَا قَدْ شَذَّ عَنْكَ سَلِ

وَقَدْ قِيلَ: الْكَسَلُ مِنْ قِلَّةِ التَّأَمُّلِ فِي مَنَاقِبِ الْعِلْمِ وَفَضَائِلِهِ، فَيَنْبَغِي أَنْ يُتْعِبَ نَفْسَهُ عَلَى التَّحْصِيلِ وَالْجِدِّ وَالْمُوَاظَبَةِ بِالتَّأَمُّلِ فِي فَضَائِلِ الْعِلْمِ، فَإِنَّ الْعِلْمَ يَبْقَىٰ [بِبَقَاءِ الْمَعْلُومَاتِ]، وَالْمَالَ يَفْنَى، كَمَا قَالَ أَمِيرُ الْمُؤْمِنِينَ عَلِيُّ بْنُ أَبِي طَالِبٍ كَرَّمَ اللَّهُ وَجْهَهُ:

رَضِينَا قِسْمَةَ الْجَبَّارِ فِينَا      لَنَا عِلْمٌ وَلِلْأَعْدَاءِ مَالُ
فَإِنَّ الْمَالَ يَفْنَىٰ عَنْ قَرِيبٍ      وَإِنَّ الْعِلْمَ يَبْقَىٰ لَا يَزَالُ

وَالْعِلْمُ النَّافِعُ يَحْصُلُ بِهِ حُسْنُ الذِّكْرِ وَيَبْقَىٰ ذَلِكَ بَعْدَ وَفَاتِهِ، وَإِنَّهُ حَيَاةٌ أَبَدِيَّةٌ.

وَأَنْشَدَنَا الشَّيْخُ الْإِمَامُ الْأَجَلُّ ظَهِيرُ الدِّينِ مُفْتِي الْأَئِمَّةِ الْحَسَنُ بْنُ عَلِيٍّ الْمَعْرُوفُ بِالْمَرْغِينَانِيِّ:

الْجَاهِلُونَ مَوْتَى قَبْلَ مَوْتِهِمُ      وَالْعَالِمُونَ وَإِنْ مَاتُوا فَأَحْيَاءُ

وَأَنْشَدَنِي الشَّيْخُ الْإِمَامُ الْأَجَلُّ بُرْهَانُ الدِّينِ رَحِمَهُ اللَّهُ:

وَفِي الْجَهْلِ قَبْلَ الْمَوْتِ مَوْتٌ لِأَهْلِهِ      فَأَجْسَامُهُمْ قَبْلَ الْقُبُورِ قُبُورُ
وَإِنِ امْرُؤٌ لَمْ يَحْيَا بِالْعِلْمِ مَيِّتٌ      فَلَيْسَ لَهُ حِينَ النُّشُورِ نُشُورُ

*A person of knowledge lives on after his death,*
*Even if his body is reduced to dust beneath the soil.*
*But an ignorant person is dead whilst walking on the earth,*
*Appearing among the living, but truly lifeless.*

Another said:

*The life of the heart is knowledge – so seize it,*
*The death of the heart is ignorance – so shun it.*

Our teacher, Shaykh al-Islām, Burhān al-Dīn ؒ recited:

*This knowledge is the highest rank in all stations,*
*And beneath it, nobility's pride is fleeting in parades.*
*The honour of a knowledgeable one grows ever stronger,*
*While the ignorant, after death, lie beneath the waves.*
*Far beyond reach is its scope for one who ascends,*
*Even for the sovereign of kingdoms or leader of troops.*
*I shall impart to you some of its merits, so listen,*
*For I cannot encompass all its virtues in these words.*
*It is light – pure light – that guides away from blindness,*
*While the ignorant wander through the darkness of ages.*
*It is the lofty summit that shelters those who seek refuge,*
*Granting them peace amidst the trials of calamities.*
*Through it, people are honoured even in their heedlessness;*
*Through it, hope is found as life clings to its essence.*
*Through it, the sinner gains intercession,*
*Rescued from the depths of Hell's dreadful end.*
*Whoever seeks it seeks all aspirations,*
*Whoever attains it attains all ambitions.*
*It is the highest station, O companion of intellect;*
*If you achieve it, consider all other ranks insignificant.*
*If the world and its fleeting delights escape you,*
*Close your eyes, for knowledge is the best of all gifts.*

It is said in this meaning:

*If a scholar takes pride in knowledge,*

وَقَالَ غَيْرُهُ:

أَخُو الْعِلْمِ حَيٌّ خَالِدٌ بَعْدَ مَوْتِهِ    وَأَوْصَالُهُ تَحْتَ التُّرَابِ رَمِيمُ
وَذُو الْجَهْلِ مَيْتٌ وَهُوَ يَمْشِي عَلَى الثَّرَ    ى يُظَنُّ مِنَ الْأَحْيَاءِ وَهُوَ عَدِيمُ

وَقَالَ آخَرُ:

حَيَاةُ الْقَلْبِ عِلْمٌ فَاغْتَنِمْهُ    وَمَوْتُ الْقَلْبِ جَهْلٌ فَاجْتَنِبْهُ

وَأَنْشَدَنِي أُسْتَاذُنَا شَيْخُ الْإِسْلَامِ بُرْهَانُ الدِّينِ رَحْمَةُ اللهِ عَلَيْهِ:

ذَا الْعِلْمِ أَعْلَى رُتْبَةً فِي الْمَرَاتِبِ    وَمَنْ دُونَهُ عِزُّ الْعُلَى فِي الْمَوَاكِبِ
فَذُو الْعِلْمِ يَبْقَى عِزُّهُ مُتَضَاعِفًا    وَذُو الْجُهْلِ بَعْدَ الْمَوْتِ تَحْتَ التَّيَارِبِ
فَهَيْهَاتَ لَا يَرْجُو مَدَاهُ مَنِ ارْتَقَى    رُقِي وَلِيِّ الْمُلْكِ وَالِي الْكَتَائِبِ
سَأُمْلِي عَلَيْكُمْ بَعْضَ مَا فِيهِ فَاسْمَعُوا    فَبِي حَصْرٌ عَنْ ذِكْرِ كُلِّ الْمَنَاقِبِ
هُوَ النُّورُ كُلُّ النُّورِ يَهْدِي عَنِ الْعَمَى    وَذُو الْجُهْلِ مَرَّ الدَّهْرِ بَيْنَ الْغَيَاهِبِ
هُوَ الذِّرْوَةُ الشَّمَّاءُ تَحْمِي مَنِ الْتَجَا    إِلَيْهَا وَيُمْسِي آمِنًا فِي النَّوَائِبِ
بِهِ [يُنْتَخَى] وَالنَّاسُ فِي غَفَلَاتِهِمْ    بِهِ يُرْتَجَى وَالرُّوحُ بَيْنَ التَّرَائِبِ
بِهِ يَشْفَعُ الْإِنْسَانُ مَنْ رَاحَ عَاصِيًا    إِلَى دَرَكِ النِّيرَانِ شَرِّ الْعَوَاقِبِ
فَمَنْ رَامَهُ رَامَ الْمَآرِبَ كُلَّهَا    وَمَنْ حَازَهُ قَدْ حَازَ كُلَّ الْمَطَالِبِ
هُوَ الْمَنْصِبُ الْعَالِي يَا صَاحِبَ الْحِجَا    إِذَا نِلْتَهُ هَوِّنْ بِفَوْتِ الْمَنَاصِبِ
فَإِنْ فَاتَكَ الدُّنْيَا وَطِيبُ نَعِيمِهَا    فَغَمِّضْ فَإِنَّ الْعِلْمَ خَيْرُ الْمَوَاهِبِ

وَقِيلَ فِي هَذَا الْمَعْنَى:

إِذَا مَا اعْتَزَّ ذُو عِلْمٍ بِعِلْمٍ    فَعِلْمُ الْفِقْهِ أَوْلَى بِاعْتِزَازِ
فَكَمْ طِيبٍ يَفُوحُ وَلَا كَمِسْكٍ    وَكَمْ طَيْرٍ يَطِيرُ وَلَا كَبَازِ

*The knowledge of fiqh deserves the greatest pride.*
*For what fragrance compares to musk?*
*And what bird soars higher than a hawk?*

Another recited:

*Knowledge is the most precious treasure you can amass;*
*Whoever studies knowledge, their virtues are not forgotten.*
*Strive to learn what you have become ignorant of;*
*The beginning of knowledge is engagement, and its end is mastery.*

The joy of knowledge, understanding, and comprehension is sufficient to inspire and motivate an intelligent person to pursue it. It is said that laziness can arise from an excess of phlegm and moisture, which can be reduced by eating less.

Seventy physicians reportedly agreed that forgetfulness stems from excess phlegm, which results from drinking too much water, caused by overeating. Dry bread cuts phlegm, as does eating raisins on an empty stomach (though not excessively), to avoid needing water, which increases phlegm.

Using *siwāk* reduces phlegm, improves memory and eloquence, and is a Sunnah practice. It increases the reward of prayer and Qur'an recitation. Vomiting also reduces phlegm and moisture. The way to reduce overeating is to reflect on the benefits of eating less, which include health, chastity, and altruism.

It is said regarding it:

*Shame, shame, and more shame! For a man's illness is caused by food.*

The Prophet ﷺ said: "Three people are hated by Allah without sin: the glutton, the miser, and the arrogant." Reflect on the harms of overeating: diseases and mental dullness. It is said: "Gluttony extinguishes intelligence."

Gālīnūs (Galen) said: "Pomegranates are wholly beneficial,

وَأُنْشِدْتُ أَيْضًا لِبَعْضِهِمْ:

الْفِقْهُ أَنْفَسُ كُلِّ شَيْءٍ أَنْتَ ذَاخِرُهُ مَنْ يَدْرُسِ الْعِلْمَ لَمْ تَدْرُسْ مَفَاخِرُهُ
فَاكْسَبْ لِنَفْسِكَ مَا أَصْبَحْتَ تَجْهَلُهُ فَأَوَّلُ الْعِلْمِ إِقْبَالٌ وَآخِرُهُ

وَكَفَىٰ بِلَذَّةِ الْعِلْمِ وَالْفِقْهِ وَالْفَهْمِ دَاعِيًا وَبَاعِثًا لِلْعَاقِلِ عَلَىٰ تَحْصِيلِ الْعِلْمِ.

وَقَدْ يَتَوَلَّدُ الْكَسَلُ مِنْ كَثْرَةِ الْبَلْغَمِ وَالرُّطُوبَاتِ، وَطَرِيقُ تَقْلِيلِهِ، تَقْلِيلُ الطَّعَامِ.

قِيلَ: اتَّفَقَ سَبْعُونَ [طَبِيبًا] عَلَىٰ أَنَّ النِّسْيَانَ مِنْ كَثْرَةِ الْبَلْغَمِ، وَكَثْرَةُ الْبَلْغَمِ مِنْ كَثْرَةِ شُرْبِ الْمَاءِ، وَكَثْرَةُ شُرْبِ الْمَاءِ مِنْ كَثْرَةِ الأَكْلِ، وَالْخُبْزُ الْيَابِسُ يَقْطَعُ الْبَلْغَمَ، وَكَذٰلِكَ أَكْلُ الزَّبِيبِ عَلَى الرِّيقِ، وَلَا يُكْثِرُ مِنْهُ، حَتَّىٰ لَا يَحْتَاجَ إِلَىٰ شُرْبِ الْمَاءِ فَيَزِيدُ الْبَلْغَمَ.

وَالسِّوَاكُ يُقَلِّلُ الْبَلْغَمَ، وَيَزِيدُ فِي الْحِفْظِ وَالْفَصَاحَةِ، فَإِنَّهُ سُنَّةٌ سَنِيَّةٌ، تَزِيدُ فِي ثَوَابِ الصَّلَاةِ، وَقِرَاءَةِ الْقُرْآنِ، وَكَذَا الْقَيْءُ يُقَلِّلُ الْبَلْغَمَ وَالرُّطُوبَاتِ، وَطَرِيقُ تَقْلِيلِ الْأَكْلِ التَّأَمُّلُ فِي مَنَافِعِ قِلَّةِ الْأَكْلِ وَهِيَ: الصِّحَّةُ وَالْعِفَّةُ وَالإِيثَارُ. وَقِيلَ فِيهِ:

فَعَارٌ ثُمَّ عَارٌ ثُمَّ عَارٌ سَقَامُ الْمَرْءِ مِنْ أَجْلِ الطَّعَامِ

وَعَنِ النَّبِيِّ عَلَيْهِ السَّلَامُ أَنَّهُ قَالَ: «ثَلَاثَةٌ يُبْغِضُهُمُ اللَّهُ مِنْ غَيْرِ جُرْمٍ: الْأَكُولُ وَالْبَخِيلُ وَالْمُتَكَبِّرُ».

وَتَأَمَّلْ فِي مَضَارِّ كَثْرَةِ الْأَكْلِ وَهِيَ: الْأَمْرَاضُ وَكَلَالَةُ الطَّبْعِ، وَقِيلَ:

while fish is wholly harmful. A small amount of fish is better than a large amount of pomegranates."

Overeating also wastes wealth. Eating beyond satiety is pure harm and incurs punishment in the Hereafter. The glutton is despised in people's hearts. To reduce eating, one should eat rich foods sparingly and begin with lighter, more palatable foods. Do not eat with the hungry unless there is a valid need, such as preparing for fasting, prayer, or arduous tasks. In such cases, it is permissible.

الْبِطْنَةُ تُذْهِبُ الْفِطْنَةَ.

حُكِيَ عَنْ جَالِينُوسٍ أَنَّهُ قَالَ : الرُّمَّانُ نَفْعٌ كُلُّهُ، وَالسَّمَكُ ضَرَرٌ كُلُّهُ، وَقَلِيلُ السَّمَكِ خَيْرٌ مِنْ كَثِيرِ الرُّمَّانِ.

وَفِيهِ أَيْضًا: إِتْلَافُ الْمَالِ، وَالْأَكْلُ فَوْقَ الشِّبَعِ ضَرَرٌ مَحْضٌ وَيُسْتَحَقُّ بِهِ الْعِقَابُ فِي دَارِ الْآخِرَةِ، وَالْأَكُولُ بَغِيضٌ فِي الْقُلُوبِ.

وَطَرِيقُ تَقْلِيلِ الْأَكْلِ : أَنْ يَأْكُلَ الْأَطْعِمَةَ الدَّسِمَةَ وَيُقَدِّمَ فِي الْأَكْلِ الْأَلْطَفَ وَالْأَشْهَىٰ، وَلَا يَأْكُلَ مَعَ الْجَائِعِ إِلَّا إِذَا كَانَ لَهُ غَرَضٌ صَحِيحٌ فِي كَثْرَةِ الْأَكْلِ بِأَنْ يَتَقَوَّىٰ بِهِ عَلَى الصِّيَامِ وَالصَّلَاةِ وَالْأَعْمَالِ الشَّاقَّةِ فَلَهُ ذَلِكَ.

## THE COMMENCEMENT OF STUDY, ITS SCOPE, AND ITS ORGANISATION

Our teacher, Shaykh al-Islām, Burḥān al-Dīn ﷺ would begin studies on Wednesdays. He would narrate a Hadith as evidence, saying: "The Messenger of Allah ﷺ said: 'Nothing begins on a Wednesday except that it is completed.' This was also the practice of my father." He narrated this Hadith from his teacher, Shaykh Imām Qiwām al-Dīn Aḥmad ibn 'Abd al-Rashīd ﷺ. I also heard from a trusted source that Shaykh Yūsuf al-Ḥamadhānī ﷺ would reserve all virtuous deeds to be started on Wednesdays. This was because Wednesday is the day on which light was created, and while it is a day of ill omen for disbelievers, it is considered blessed for believers.

As for the scope of study at the outset, Abū Ḥanīfah ﷺ is reported to have quoted Shaykh Qāḍī Imām 'Umar ibn Abī Bakr al-Zarnajārī ﷺ, who said: "Our elders ﷺ would recommend that the beginner should undertake as much as he can memorise with repetition twice, gently. Each day, they would increase by one word so that, even if the study lengthened and the material increased, it could still be mastered with two repetitions. They would increase gradually and methodically. If the study became too lengthy at the beginning and required ten repetitions, the same habit would persist at later stages, as it would become ingrained and would only be abandoned with great effort. It is said: 'Study is a single letter, and repetition is a thousand letters.'"

One should start with material that is closer to one's understanding. Shaykh Imām Ustādh Sharaf al-Dīn al-'Uqaylī ﷺ said: "In my opinion, the correct approach is what our elders practised, as they would select the smaller sections of *Al-Mabsūṭ* for beginners. This is because it is easier to understand, retain, and less likely to induce boredom while also being more relevant to common practice."

## فَصلٌ: فِي بِدَايَةِ السَّبَقِ وَقَدْرِهِ وَتَرْتِيبِهِ

كَانَ أُسْتَاذُنَا شَيْخُ الْإِسْلَامِ بُرْهَانُ الدِّينِ رَحِمَهُ اللّٰهُ يُوقِفُ بِدَايَةَ السَّبَقِ عَلَىٰ يَوْمِ الْأَرْبعَاءِ، وَكَانَ يَرْوِي فِي ذَلِكَ حَدِيثًا وَيَسْتَدِلُّ بِهِ وَيَقُولُ: قَالَ رَسُولُ اللهِ ﷺ: «مَا مِنْ شَيْءٍ بُدِئَ يَوْمَ الْأَرْبعَاءِ إِلَّا وَقَدْ تَمَّ»، وَهَكَذَا كَانَ يَفْعَلُ أَبِي. وَكَانَ يَرْوِي هٰذَا الْحَدِيثَ عَنْ أُسْتَاذِهِ الشَّيْخِ الْإِمَامِ الْأَجَلِّ قِوَامِ الدِّينِ أَحْمَدَ بْنِ عَبْدِ الرَّشِيدِ رَحِمَهُ اللّٰهُ. وَسَمِعْتُ مِمَّنْ أَثِقُ بِهِ، أَنَّ الشَّيْخَ يُوسُفَ الْهَمَذَانِيَّ رَحِمَهُ اللّٰهُ، كَانَ يُوقِفُ كُلَّ عَمَلٍ مِنْ أَعْمَالِ الْخَيْرِ عَلَىٰ يَوْمِ الْأَرْبعَاءِ؛ وَهٰذَا لِأَنَّ يَوْمَ الْأَرْبعَاءِ يَوْمٌ خُلِقَ فِيهِ النُّورُ، وَهُوَ يَوْمُ نَحْسٍ فِي حَقِّ الْكُفَّارِ فَيَكُونُ مُبَارَكًا لِلْمُؤْمِنِينَ. وَأَمَّا قَدْرُ السَّبَقِ فِي الِابْتِدَاءِ: كَانَ [أَبُو حَنِيفَةَ رَحِمَهُ اللّٰهُ] يَحْكِي عَنِ الشَّيْخِ الْقَاضِي الْإِمَامِ عُمَرَ بْنِ أَبِي بَكْرٍ الزَّرْنَجَرِيِّ رَحِمَهُ اللّٰهُ أَنَّهُ قَالَ: قَالَ مَشَايِخُنَا رَحِمَهُمُ اللّٰهُ: يَنْبَغِي أَنْ يَكُونَ قَدْرُ السَّبَقِ لِلْمُبْتَدِي قَدْرُ مَا يُمْكِنُ ضَبْطُهُ بِالْإِعَادَةِ مَرَّتَيْنِ بِالرِّفْقِ، وَيَزِيدُ كُلَّ يَوْمٍ كَلِمَةً حَتَّىٰ أَنَّهُ وَإِنْ طَالَ وَكَثُرَ يُمْكِنُ ضَبْطُهُ بِالْإِعَادَةِ مَرَّتَيْنِ، وَيَزِيدُ بِالرِّفْقِ وَالتَّدْرِيجِ، وَأَمَّا إِذَا طَالَ السَّبَقُ فِي الِابْتِدَاءِ وَاحْتَاجَ إِلَى الْإِعَادَةِ عَشْرَ مَرَّاتٍ فَهُوَ فِي الِانْتِهَاءِ أَيْضًا يَكُونُ كَذَلِكَ، لِأَنَّهُ يَعْتَادُ ذَلِكَ، وَلَا يَتْرُكُ تِلْكَ الْعَادَةَ إِلَّا بِجُهْدٍ كَثِيرٍ، وَقَدْ قِيلَ: السَّبَقُ حَرْفٌ، وَالتَّكْرَارُ أَلْفٌ. وَيَنْبَغِي أَنْ يَبْتَدِئَ بِشَيْءٍ يَكُونُ أَقْرَبَ إِلَىٰ فَهْمِهِ، وَكَانَ الشَّيْخُ الإِمَامُ الْأُسْتَاذُ شَرَفُ الدِّينِ الْعُقَيْلِيُّ رَحِمَهُ اللّٰهُ

After achieving comprehension and thorough repetition, the material should be reviewed extensively, as this is highly beneficial. A student should not write down anything they do not understand, as doing so leads to mental fatigue, dullness of wit, and wasted time.

The student should strive to comprehend the teacher's lessons through reflection, thought, and frequent repetition. If the amount of material is small, yet the repetition and reflection are abundant, comprehension will be achieved. It is said: "Memorising two letters is better than hearing two sacks [of knowledge], and understanding two letters is better than memorising two sacks."

If one neglects understanding and fails to exert effort once or twice, this habit will persist, and even simple matters will become incomprehensible. Thus, one must not neglect understanding but should strive and supplicate to Allah with humility, as He answers those who call upon Him and does not disappoint those who place their hope in Him.

Shaykh al-Ajall Qiwām al-Dīn Ḥammād ibn Ibrāhīm al-Ṣaffār al-Anṣārī ﷺ recited to us, dictated by Qāḍī Khalīl ibn Aḥmad al-Shajarī:

*Serve knowledge as one seeking benefit,*
*And maintain its study with praiseworthy actions.*
*Whenever you memorise something, review it,*
*Then reinforce it to the utmost degree.*
*Annotate it so you may return to it,*
*And persist in its study forevermore.*
*When you are secure from losing it,*
*Proceed to something new.*
*Yet continue repeating what preceded,*
*While acquiring more of this great endeavour.*
*Discuss knowledge with others to keep it alive;*
*Do not be distant from people of understanding.*
*If you conceal knowledge, you will forget it,*

يَقُولُ: الصَّوَابُ عِنْدِي فِي هٰذا مَا فَعَلَهُ مَشَايِخُنَا رَحِمَهُمُ اللَّهُ، فَإِنَّهُمْ كَانُوا يَخْتَارُونَ لِلْمُبْتَدِئِ صِغَارَاتِ الْمَبْسُوطِ؛ لِأَنَّهُ أَقْرَبُ إِلَى الْفَهْمِ وَالضَّبْطِ، وَأَبْعَدُ مِنَ الْمَلَالَةِ، وَأَكْثَرُ وُقُوعًا بَيْنَ النَّاسِ. **وَيَنْبَغِي** أَنْ يُعَلِّقَ السَّبَقَ بَعْدَ الضَّبْطِ وَالْإِعَادَةِ كَثِيرًا، فَإِنَّهُ نَافِعٌ جِدًّا. وَلَا يَكْتُبُ الْمُتَعَلِّمُ شَيْئًا لَا يَفْهَمُهُ، فَإِنَّهُ يُورِثُ كَلَالَةَ الطَّبْعِ وَيُذْهِبُ الْفِطْنَةَ وَيَضَيِّعُ أَوْقَاتَهُ. **وَيَنْبَغِي** أَنْ يَجْتَهِدَ فِي الْفَهْمِ عَنِ الْأَسْتَاذِ بِالتَّأَمُّلِ وَالتَّفَكُّرِ وَكَثْرَةِ التَّكْرَارِ، فَإِنَّهُ إِذَا قَلَّ السَّبَقُ وَكَثُرَ التَّكْرَارُ وَالتَّأَمُّلُ يُدْرِكُ وَيَفْهَمُ. قِيلَ: حِفْظُ حَرْفَيْنِ، خَيْرٌ مِنْ سَمَاعِ وَقْرَيْنِ، وَفَهْمُ حَرْفَيْنِ خَيْرٌ مِنْ حِفْظِ وَقْرَيْنِ. **وَإِذَا تَهَاوَنَ** فِي الْفَهْمِ وَلَمْ يَجْتَهِدْ مَرَّةً أَوْ مَرَّتَيْنِ يَعْتَادُ ذَلِكَ فَلَا يَفْهَمُ الْكَلَامَ الْيَسِيرَ، فَيَنْبَغِي أَنْ لَا يَتَهَاوَنَ فِي الْفَهْمِ؛ بَلْ يَجْتَهِدَ وَيَدْعُوَ اللَّهَ وَيَتَضَرَّعَ إِلَيْهِ فَإِنَّهُ يُجِيبُ مَنْ دَعَاهُ، وَلَا يُخَيِّبُ مَنْ رَجَاهُ. **وَأَنْشَدَنَا** الشَّيْخُ الْأَجَلُّ قِوَامُ الدِّينِ حَمَّادُ بْنُ إِبْرَاهِيمَ بْنُ إِسْمَاعِيلَ الصَّفَّارُ الْأَنْصَارِيُّ إِمْلَاءً لِلْقَاضِي الْخَلِيلِ بْنِ أَحْمَدَ الشَّجْرِيِّ فِي ذَلِكَ:

اخْدُمِ الْعِلْمَ خِدْمَةَ الْمُسْتَفِيدِ ... وَأَدِمْ دَرْسَهُ بِفِعْلٍ حَمِيدِ
وَإِذَا مَا حَفِظْتَ شَيْئًا فَأَعِدْهُ ... ثُمَّ أَكِّدْهُ غَايَةَ التَّأْكِيدِ
ثُمَّ عَلِّقْهُ كَيْ تَعُودَ إِلَيْهِ ... وَإِلَى دَرْسِهِ عَلَى التَّأْبِيدِ
فَإِذَا مَا أَمِنْتَ مِنْهُ فَوَاتًا ... فَانْتَدِبْ بَعْدَهُ بِشَيْءٍ جَدِيدِ
مَعَ تَكْرَارِ مَا تَقَدَّمَ مِنْهُ ... وَاقْتِنَاءً لِشَأْنِ هٰذَا الْمَزِيدِ
ذَاكِرِ النَّاسَ بِالْعُلُومِ لِتَحْيَى ... لَا تَكُنْ مِنْ أُولِي النُّهَى بِبَعِيدِ

*Until you are seen as ignorant and dull*
*Then, on the Day of Resurrection, you will be muzzled with fire*
*And engulfed in severe torment.*

A student of knowledge must engage in review, debate, and exchange of ideas. These should be conducted with fairness, patience, and careful thought. One must avoid contentiousness and anger, as debate and discussion are forms of consultation, and consultation is meant to uncover the truth. This is only achieved with patience, reflection, and fairness – not with anger and argumentation.

If one's intention in discussion is merely to dominate or defeat one's opponent, this is impermissible. The only permissible intention is to reveal the truth. Deception and trickery are not allowed in these matters unless the opponent is obstinate and not genuinely seeking the truth.

Muhammad ibn Yaḥyā, when faced with a difficulty and unable to find an answer, would say: "What you have imposed upon me is valid, and I am reflecting on it. Above every possessor of knowledge is One All-Knowing."

The benefit of exchanging ideas and debating is greater than mere repetition because it involves both repetition and an increase in understanding.

And it was said: "An hour of discussion is better than a month of repetition, but only when it is with someone fair and of sound temperament."

Beware of engaging in discussions with a contentious person who lacks upright character, for temperaments are influential, morals are transferable, and proximity has an impact.

The poetry mentioned by Khalīl ibn Aḥmad contains numerous benefits. It is said:

*Knowledge demands from its seeker*
*That he treats all people as its servants.*

A student of knowledge must always reflect on the subtleties

إِنْ كَتَمْتَ الْعُلُومَ أُنْسِيتَ حَتَّى لَا تُرَىٰ غَيْرَ جَاهِلٍ وَبَلِيدِ
ثُمَّ أُلْجِمْتَ فِي الْقِيَامَةِ نَارًا وَتَلَهَّبْتَ بِالْعَذَابِ الشَّدِيدِ

وَلَا بُدَّ لِطَالِبِ الْعِلْمِ مِنَ الْمُذَاكَرَةِ، وَالْمُنَاظَرَةِ، وَالْمُطَارَحَةِ، فَيَنْبَغِي أَنْ يَكُونَ كُلٌّ مِنْهَا بِالْإِنْصَافِ وَالتَّأَنِّي وَالتَّأَمُّلِ، وَيَتَحَرَّزَ عَنِ الشَّغَبِ وَالغَضَبِ، فَإِنَّ الْمُنَاظَرَةَ وَالْمُذَاكَرَةَ مُشَاوَرَةٌ، وَالْمُشَاوَرَةُ إِنَّمَا تَكُونُ لِاسْتِخْرَاجِ الصَّوَابِ، وَذَلِكَ إِنَّمَا يَحْصُلُ بِالتَّأَنِّي وَالتَّأَمُّلِ وَالْإِنْصَافِ، وَلَا يَحْصُلُ بِالغَضَبِ وَالشَّغَبِ.

فَإِنْ كَانَتْ نِيَّتُهُ مِنَ الْمُبَاحَثَةِ إِلْزَامُ الخَصْمِ وَقَهْرُهُ، فَلَا يَحِلُّ ذَلِكَ، وَإِنَّمَا يَحِلُّ ذَلِكَ لِإِظْهَارِ الحَقِّ.

وَالتَّمْوِيهُ وَالحِيلَةُ لَا يَجُوزُ فِيهَا، إِلَّا إِذَا كَانَ الخَصْمُ مُتَعَنِّتًا، لَا طَالِبًا لِلْحَقِّ. وَكَانَ مُحَمَّدُ بْنُ يَحْيَىٰ إِذَا تَوَجَّهَ عَلَيْهِ الإِشْكَالُ، وَلَمْ يَحْضُرْهُ الجَوَابُ يَقُولُ: مَا أَلْزَمْتُهُ لَازِمٌ، وَأَنَا فِيهِ نَاظِرٌ، وَفَوْقَ كُلِّ ذِي عِلْمٍ عَلِيمٌ. وَفَائِدَةُ الْمُطَارَحَةِ وَالْمُنَاظَرَةِ أَقْوَىٰ مِنْ فَائِدَةِ مُجَرَّدِ التَّكْرَارِ؛ لِأَنَّ فِيهِ تَكْرَارًا وَزِيَادَةً. **وَقِيلَ**: مُطَارَحَةُ سَاعَةٍ، خَيْرٌ مِنْ تَكْرَارِ شَهْرٍ؛ لَكِنْ إِذَا كَانَ مَعَ مُنْصِفٍ سَلِيمِ الطَّبِيعَةِ. وَإِيَّاكَ وَالْمُذَاكَرَةَ مَعَ مُتَعَنِّتٍ غَيْرِ مُسْتَقِيمِ الطَّبْعِ، فَإِنَّ الطَّبِيعَةَ مُتَسَرِّيَةٌ، وَالْأَخْلَاقَ مُتَعَدِّيَةٌ، وَالْمُجَاوَرَةُ مُؤَثِّرَةٌ. وَفِي الشِّعْرِ الَّذِي ذَكَرَهُ الخَلِيلُ بْنُ أَحْمَدَ فَوَائِدُ كَثِيرَةٌ، قِيلَ:

الْعِلْمُ مِنْ شَرْطِهِ لِمَنْ خَدَمَهُ أَنْ يَجْعَلَ النَّاسَ كُلَّهُمْ خَدَمَهُ

of knowledge, in all states and times, until this becomes a habit. This is because subtle insights are only attained through reflection. Hence, it is said: "Reflect, and you will attain."

One must also reflect before speaking, so one's words are accurate. Speech is like an arrow – it must be aligned through reflection before being released to hit its mark.

It is mentioned in the principles of jurisprudence that this is a major principle: the speech of a jurist in debate must be deliberate. It is said: "The pinnacle of intellect is that speech is founded upon deliberation and reflection."

A wise man said:

*I counsel you in crafting your speech with five points,*
*If you wish to heed the advice of a sincere advisor:*
*Do not overlook the cause of your speech or its timing,*
*And its manner, measure, and place altogether.*

One should strive to benefit from all circumstances and times and from all people. The Messenger of Allah ﷺ said: "Wisdom is the lost property of the believer; wherever he finds it, he takes it." He ﷺ also said: "Take what is pure and leave what is impure."

I heard Shaykh Imām al-Ajall al-Ustādh Fakhr al-Dīn al-Kāshānī say: "There was a maidservant of Abū Yūsuf entrusted to Muhammad [ibn al-Ḥasan]. She was asked: 'Do you recall anything of Abū Yūsuf's jurisprudence?' She replied: 'No, except that he often repeated and said: *The share of rotation is void.*' Muhammad memorised this from her, and it resolved a complex issue that had troubled him. From this, we learn that benefit can come from anyone."

For this reason, when Abū Yūsuf was asked: "How did you attain knowledge?" he replied: "I never disdained learning from anyone, nor was I stingy in imparting knowledge."

Ibn 'Abbās ﷺ was asked: "How did you attain knowledge?" He replied: "With a questioning tongue and a comprehending

وَيَنْبَغِي لِطَالِبِ الْعِلْمِ أَنْ يَكُونَ مُتَأَمِّلًا فِي جَمِيعِ الْأَوْقَاتِ فِي دَقَائِقِ الْعُلُومِ، وَيَعْتَادَ ذَلِكَ، فَإِنَّمَا يُدْرِكُ الدَّقَائِقَ بِالتَّأَمُّلِ، فَلِهَذَا قِيلَ: تَأَمَّلْ تُدْرِكْ. وَلَا بُدَّ مِنَ التَّأَمُّلِ قَبْلَ الْكَلَامِ حَتَّى يَكُونَ صَوَابًا، فَإِنَّ الْكَلَامَ كَالسَّهْمِ، فَلَا بُدَّ مِنْ تَقْوِيمِهِ بِالتَّأَمُّلِ قَبْلَ الْكَلَامِ حَتَّى يَكُونَ مُصِيبًا.

وَقَالَ فِي أُصُولِ الْفِقْهِ: هَذَا أَصْلٌ كَبِيرٌ، وَهُوَ أَنْ يَكُونَ كَلَامُ الْفَقِيهِ الْمُنَاظِرِ بِالتَّأَمُّلِ.

قِيلَ: رَأْسُ الْعَقْلِ أَنْ يَكُونَ الْكَلَامُ بِالتَّثَبُّتِ وَالتَّأَمُّلِ. قَالَ قَائِلٌ:

أُوصِيكَ فِي نَظْمِ الْكَلَامِ بِخَمْسَةٍ ... إِنْ كُنْتَ لِلْمُوصِي الشَّفِيقِ مُطِيعَا
لَا تُغْفِلَنَّ سَبَبَ الْكَلَامِ وَوَقْتَهُ ... وَالْكَيْفَ وَالْكَمَّ وَالْمَكَانَ جَمِيعَا

وَيَكُونَ مُسْتَفِيدًا فِي جَمِيعِ الْأَحْوَالِ وَالْأَوْقَاتِ مِنْ جَمِيعِ الْأَشْخَاصِ، قَالَ رَسُولُ اللَّهِ ﷺ: «الْحِكْمَةُ ضَالَّةُ الْمُؤْمِنِ، أَيْنَمَا وَجَدَهَا أَخَذَهَا». وَقِيلَ : خُذْ مَا صَفَا، وَدَعْ مَا كَدَرَ. وَسَمِعْتُ الشَّيْخَ الْإِمَامَ الْأَجَلَّ الْأُسْتَاذَ فَخْرَ الدِّينِ الْكَاشَانِيَّ يَقُولُ: كَانَتْ جَارِيَةٌ لِأَبِي يُوسُفَ أَمَانَةٌ عِنْدَ مُحَمَّدٍ [بْنِ الْحَسَنِ] فَقَالَ لَهَا : هَلْ تَحْفَظِينَ [مِنْ] أَبِي يُوسُفَ فِي الْفِقْهِ شَيْئًا؟ فَقَالَتْ: لَا، إِلَّا أَنَّهُ كَانَ يُكَرِّرُ وَيَقُولُ: سَهْمُ الدَّوْرِ سَاقِطٌ. فَحَفِظَ ذَلِكَ مِنْهَا، وَكَانَتْ تِلْكَ الْمَسْأَلَةُ مُشْكِلَةً عَلَى مُحَمَّدٍ فَارْتَفَعَ إِشْكَالُهُ بِهَذِهِ الْكَلِمَةِ. فَعُلِمَ أَنَّ الِاسْتِفَادَةَ مُمْكِنَةٌ مِنْ كُلِّ أَحَدٍ. وَلِهَذَا قَالَ أَبُو يُوسُفَ حِينَ قِيلَ لَهُ: بِمَا أَدْرَكْتَ الْعِلْمَ؟ فَقَالَ: مَا

heart." In earlier times, a student of knowledge was often called *What do you say?* because people would frequently ask: *What do you say about this issue?*

Abū Ḥanīfah ﷺ gained understanding through frequent discussions and debates in his shop while working as a cloth merchant. This shows that the pursuit of knowledge and jurisprudence can be combined with earning a livelihood.

Abū Ḥafṣ al-Kabīr used to earn a living while repeating and studying knowledge. Thus, if a student of knowledge must work to provide for his family or other needs, he should continue to study, review, and discuss without falling into laziness.

A person of sound body and mind has no excuse to abandon learning and understanding. No one was poorer than Abū Yūsuf, yet his poverty did not prevent him from seeking knowledge. Whoever possesses wealth should consider it a blessing, for a righteous person uses it to aid in the pursuit of knowledge. It is narrated that a scholar was once asked: "How did you attain knowledge?" He replied: "Through a wealthy father." This is because wealth can benefit people of knowledge and virtue by supporting their studies. Gratitude for such blessings is a means of increasing them.

It is also said that Abū Ḥanīfah ﷺ remarked: "I attained knowledge through praising [Allah] and gratitude. Whenever I understood something or succeeded in grasping jurisprudence or wisdom, I would say *Al-ḥamdulillāh* (all praise is due to Allah), and my knowledge increased."

Thus, a student of knowledge should occupy himself with gratitude through words, actions, heart, and wealth. He should acknowledge that understanding, knowledge, and success come from Allah and seek guidance from Him through supplication and humility, for Allah is the Guide of those who seek His guidance.

اسْتَنْكَفْتُ مِنَ الِاسْتِفَادَةِ مِنْ كُلِّ أَحَدٍ، وَمَا بَخِلْتُ مِنَ الْإِفَادَةِ.

وَقِيلَ لِابْنِ عَبَّاسٍ رَضِيَ اللَّهُ عَنْهُ: بِمَا أَدْرَكْتَ الْعِلْمَ؟ قَالَ: بِلِسَانٍ سَؤُولٍ، وَقَلْبٍ عَقُولٍ. وَإِنَّمَا سُمِّيَ طَالِبُ الْعِلْمِ: «مَا تَقُولُ»؛ لِكَثْرَةِ مَا يَقُولُونَ فِي الزَّمَانِ الْأَوَّلِ: «مَا تَقُولُ فِي هَذِهِ الْمَسْأَلَةِ؟». **وَإِنَّمَا** تَفَقَّهَ أَبُو حَنِيفَةَ رحمه الله بِكَثْرَةِ الْمُطَارَحَةِ وَالْمُذَاكَرَةِ فِي دُكَّانِهِ حِينَ كَانَ بَزَّازًا. فَبِهَذَا يُعْلَمُ أَنَّ تَحْصِيلَ الْعِلْمِ وَالْفِقْهِ يَجْتَمِعُ مَعَ الْكَسْبِ. **وَكَانَ** أَبُو حَفْصٍ الْكَبِيرُ يَكْتَسِبُ وَيُكَرِّرُ الْعُلُومَ، فَإِنْ كَانَ لَا بُدَّ لِطَالِبِ الْعِلْمِ مِنَ الْكَسْبِ لِنَفَقَةِ الْعِيَالِ وَغَيْرِهِ؛ فَلْيَكْتَسِبْ وَلْيُكَرِّرْ وَلْيُذَاكِرْ وَلَا يَكْسَلْ. وَلَيْسَ لِصَحِيحِ الْبَدَنِ وَالْعَقْلِ عُذْرٌ فِي تَرْكِ التَّعَلُّمِ وَالتَّفَقُّهِ، فَإِنَّهُ لَا يَكُونُ أَفْقَرَ مِنْ أَبِي يُوسُفَ، وَلَمْ يَمْنَعْهُ ذَلِكَ مِنَ التَّفَقُّهِ؛ فَمَنْ كَانَ لَهُ مَالٌ كَثِيرٌ فَنِعْمَ الْمَالُ الصَّالِحُ لِلرَّجُلِ الصَّالِحِ، الْمُنْصَرِفِ فِي طَرِيقِ الْعِلْمِ. قِيلَ لِعَالِمٍ: بِمَا أَدْرَكْتَ الْعِلْمَ؟ قَالَ: بِأَبٍ غَنِيٍّ؛ لِأَنَّهُ كَانَ يَنْتَفِعُ بِهِ أَهْلُ الْعِلْمِ وَالْفَضْلِ، فَإِنَّهُ سَبَبُ زِيَادَةِ الْعِلْمِ؛ لِأَنَّهُ شُكْرٌ عَلَىٰ نِعْمَةِ الْعَقْلِ وَالْعِلْمِ، وَإِنَّهُ سَبَبُ الزِّيَادَةِ. **قِيلَ**: قَالَ أَبُو حَنِيفَةَ رَحِمَهُ اللَّهُ: «إِنَّمَا أَدْرَكْتُ الْعِلْمَ بِالْحَمْدِ وَالشُّكْرِ، فَكُلَّمَا فَهِمْتُ وَوُفِّقْتُ عَلَىٰ فِقْهٍ وَحِكْمَةٍ، قُلْتُ: الْحَمْدُ لِلهِ، فَازْدَادَ عِلْمِي». وَهَكَذَا يَنْبَغِي لِطَالِبِ الْعِلْمِ أَنْ يَشْتَغِلَ بِالشُّكْرِ بِاللِّسَانِ وَالْأَرْكَانِ وَالْجَنَانِ وَالْمَالِ، وَيَرَى الْفَهْمَ وَالْعِلْمَ وَالتَّوْفِيقَ مِنَ اللَّهِ تَعَالَىٰ، وَيَطْلُبَ الْهِدَايَةَ مِنَ اللَّهِ تَعَالَىٰ بِالدُّعَاءِ لَهُ وَالتَّضَرُّعِ إِلَيْهِ، فَإِنَّ اللَّهَ تَعَالَىٰ هَادٍ مَنِ اسْتَهْدَاهُ.

## THE PEOPLE OF TRUTH AND THE PEOPLE OF MISGUIDANCE

The people of truth – Ahl al-Sunnah wa al-Jamā'ah – sought the truth from Allah, the Manifest Truth, the Guiding and Protecting One, and He guided and protected them from misguidance.

The people of misguidance, however, were deluded by their opinions and intellects. They sought the truth from the creation, which is inherently incapable, such as the intellect. Just as sight cannot perceive all things, so too does the intellect fall short of comprehending everything. Thus, they were veiled, unable to attain understanding, and went astray, leading others astray.

The Messenger of Allah ﷺ said: "The heedless one acts upon his heedlessness, and the intelligent one acts upon his intellect." Acting with intellect begins with recognising one's incapacity. The Messenger of Allah ﷺ also said: "Whoever knows themselves knows their Lord." When one acknowledges one's own incapacity, one recognises Allah's power, ceases relying on oneself or one's intellect, and instead trusts in Allah, seeking the truth from Him. Whoever places his trust in Allah, He will suffice him and guide him to the Straight Path.

## WEALTH AND GENEROSITY

Whoever possesses wealth should not be stingy and should seek refuge in Allah from miserliness. The Prophet ﷺ said: "What disease is worse than miserliness?" It is reported that Abū al-Shaykh, the eminent imam, Shams al-A'immah al-Halwānī ؒ was a poor man who sold sweets. Despite his poverty, he would distribute sweets to the scholars and say: "Pray for my son." Through the blessings of his generosity, his sincerity, and his supplications to Allah, his son attained a lofty rank. He would also spend his money purchasing books and hiring

## [أَهْلُ الْحَقِّ وَأَهْلُ الْعَدَالَةِ]

فَأَهْلُ الْحَقِّ - وَهُمْ أَهْلُ السُّنَّةِ وَالْجَمَاعَةِ - طَلَبُوا الْحَقَّ مِنَ اللَّهِ تَعَالَى الْحَقِّ الْمُبِينِ الْهَادِي الْعَاصِمِ، فَهَدَاهُمُ اللَّهُ وَعَصَمَهُمْ عَنِ الضَّلَالَةِ.

وَأَهْلُ الضَّلَالَةِ أُعْجِبُوا بِرَأْيِهِمْ وَعَقْلِهِمْ، وَطَلَبُوا الْحَقَّ مِنَ الْمَخْلُوقِ الْعَاجِزِ وَهُوَ الْعَقْلُ؛ لِأَنَّ الْعَقْلَ لَا يُدْرِكُ جَمِيعَ الْأَشْيَاءِ كَالْبَصَرِ؛ [فَإِنَّهُ] لَا يُبْصِرُ جَمِيعَ الْأَشْيَاءِ فَحُجِبُوا وَعَجَزُوا عَنْ مَعْرِفَتِهِ، وَضَلُّوا وَأَضَلُّوا.

قَالَ رَسُولُ اللَّهِ ﷺ: «الْغَافِلُ مَنْ عَمِلَ بِغَفْلَتِهِ، وَالْعَاقِلُ مَنْ عَمِلَ بِعَقْلِهِ». فَالْعَمَلُ بِالْعَقْلِ أَوَّلًا: أَنْ يَعْرِفَ عَجْزَ نَفْسِهِ، قَالَ رَسُولُ اللَّهِ ﷺ: «مَنْ عَرَفَ نَفْسَهُ، فَقَدْ عَرَفَ رَبَّهُ»، فَإِذَا عَرَفَ عَجْزَ نَفْسِهِ عَرَفَ قُدْرَةَ اللَّهِ عزَّ وجلَّ، وَلَا يَعْتَمِدُ عَلَىٰ نَفْسِهِ وَعَقْلِهِ؛ بَلْ يَتَوَكَّلُ عَلَى اللَّهِ، وَيَطْلُبُ الْحَقِّ مِنْهُ، وَمَنْ يَتَوَكَّلُ عَلَى اللَّهِ فَهُوَ حَسْبُهُ وَيَهْدِيهِ إِلَىٰ صِرَاطٍ مُسْتَقِيمٍ.

وَمَنْ كَانَ لَهُ مَالٌ فَلَا يَبْخَلَ، وَيَنْبَغِي أَنْ يَتَعَوَّذَ بِاللَّهِ مِنَ الْبُخْلِ. قَالَ النَّبِيُّ عَلَيْهِ السَّلَامُ: «أَيُّ دَاءٍ أَدْوَأُ مِنَ الْبُخْلِ». وَكَانَ أَبُو الشَّيْخِ الْإِمَامُ الْأَجَلُّ شَمْسُ الْأَئِمَّةِ الْحَلْوَانِيُّ رَحِمَهُ اللَّهُ فَقِيرًا يَبِيعُ الْحَلْوَاءَ، وَكَانَ يُعْطِي الْفُقَهَاءَ مِنَ الْحَلْوَاءِ وَيَقُولُ: ادْعُوا لِابْنِي. فَبِبَرَكَةِ جُودِهِ وَاعْتِقَادِهِ وَشَفَقَتِهِ وَتَضَرُّعِهِ إِلَى اللَّهِ تَعَالَى نَالَ ابْنُهُ مَا نَالَ.

scribes to assist him in learning and gaining knowledge.

It is also narrated that Muhammad ibn al-Ḥasan owned considerable wealth, with three hundred agents managing his assets. Yet, he spent all of it in pursuit of *fiqh* and knowledge until nothing of value remained. Once, Abū Yūsuf saw him wearing a worn-out garment and sent him a set of fine clothes. However, Muhammad ibn al-Ḥasan did not accept the gift, saying: "You have been hastened your reward, while ours has been delayed." Perhaps he declined it, even though accepting gifts is a Sunnah, because he perceived it as a form of humiliation for himself.

The Messenger of Allah ﷺ said: "It is not befitting for a believer to humiliate himself."

It is also narrated that Shaykh Fakhr al-Islām al-Arsābandī ﵀ collected discarded watermelon rinds from an empty place and ate them. A servant girl saw him and informed her master, who arranged a meal and invited him. However, he declined for the same reason.

Thus, a seeker of knowledge should possess lofty ambitions and not covet people's wealth.

The Prophet ﷺ said: "Beware of greed, for it is present poverty."

Whoever possesses wealth should not withhold it but spend it on themselves and others. The Prophet ﷺ said: "People are impoverished because of their fear of poverty."

In earlier times, people would first learn a craft and then pursue knowledge to avoid dependence on others' wealth. He said: "Whoever relies on others' wealth becomes impoverished."

A scholar who is greedy undermines the sanctity of knowledge and hesitates to speak the truth. For this reason, the Prophet ﷺ sought refuge from such greed, saying: "I seek

وَيَشْتَرِي بِالْمَالِ الْكُتُبَ، وَيَسْتَكْتِبُ فَيَكُونُ عَوْنًا عَلَى التَّعَلُّمِ وَالتَّفَقُّهِ. وَقَدْ كَانَ لِمُحَمَّدِ بْنِ الْحَسَنِ مَالٌ كَثِيرٌ حَتَّى كَانَ لَهُ ثَلَاثُمِائَةٍ مِنَ الْوُكَلَاءِ عَلَىٰ مَالِهِ، وَأَنْفَقَهُ كُلَّهُ فِي الْفِقْهِ وَالْعِلْمِ، وَلَمْ يَبْقَ لَهُ ثَوْبٌ نَفِيسٌ، فَرَآهُ أَبُو يُوسُفَ فِي ثَوْبٍ خَلِقٍ، فَأَرْسَلَ إِلَيْهِ ثِيَابًا نَفِيسَةً، فَلَمْ يَقْبَلْهَا فَقَالَ: عُجِّلَ لَكُمْ، وَأُجِّلَ لَنَا. وَلَعَلَّهُ إِنَّمَا لَمْ يَقْبَلْهُ وَإِنْ كَانَ قَبُولُ الهَدِيَّةِ سُنَّةً، لِمَا رَأَىٰ فِي ذَلِكَ مَذَلَّةً لِنَفْسِهِ.

قَالَ رَسُولُ اللَّهِ عَلَيْهِ الصَّلَاةُ وَالسَّلَامُ: «لَيْسَ لِلْمُؤْمِنِ أَنْ يُذِلَّ نَفْسَهُ».

وَحُكِيَ أَنَّ الشَّيْخَ فَخْرَ الْإِسْلَامِ الْأَرْسَابَنْدِيَّ رَحِمَهُ اللَّهُ جَمَعَ قُشُورَ الْبِطِّيخِ الْمُلْقَاةِ فِي مَكَانٍ خَالٍ فَأَكَلَهَا، فَرَأَتْهُ جَارِيَةٌ فَأَخْبَرَتْ بِذَلِكَ مَوْلَاهَا، فَاتَّخَذَ لَهُ دَعْوَةً فَدَعَاهُ إِلَيْهَا، فَلَمْ يَقْبَلْ لِهَذَا.

وَهَكَذَا يَنْبَغِي لِطَالِبِ الْعِلْمِ أَنْ يَكُونَ ذَا هِمَّةٍ عَالِيَةٍ لَا يَطْمَعُ فِي أَمْوَالِ النَّاسِ. قَالَ النَّبِيُّ ﷺ: «إِيَّاكَ وَالطَّمَعَ فَإِنَّهُ فَقْرٌ حَاضِرٌ».

وَلَا يَبْخَلُ بِمَا عِنْدَهُ مِنَ الْمَالِ؛ بَلْ يُنْفِقُ عَلَىٰ نَفْسِهِ وَعَلَىٰ غَيْرِهِ.

قَالَ النَّبِيُّ عَلَيْهِ الصَّلَاةُ وَالسَّلَامُ: «النَّاسُ كُلُّهُمْ فِي الْفَقْرِ مَخَافَةَ الْفَقْرِ»، وَكَانَ فِي الزَّمَانِ الْأَوَّلِ يَتَعَلَّمُونَ الْحِرْفَةَ ثُمَّ يَتَعَلَّمُونَ الْعِلْمَ، حَتَّى لَا يَطْمَعُوا فِي أَمْوَالِ النَّاسِ.

وَفِي الْحِكْمَةِ: مَنِ اسْتَغْنَى بِمَالِ النَّاسِ افْتَقَرَ.

وَالْعَالِمُ إِذَا كَانَ طَمَّاعًا لَا يُبْقِي حُرْمَةَ الْعِلْمِ وَلَا يَقُولُ الْحَقَّ، فَلِهَذَا كَانَ يَتَعَوَّذُ صَاحِبُ الشَّرْعِ ﷺ مِنْهُ وَيَقُولُ: «أَعُوذُ بِاللَّهِ مِنْ طَمَعٍ

refuge in Allah from greed that inclines towards disgrace."[7] A believer should place his hope in none but Allah and fear none but Him. This is evident in whether he adheres to or exceeds the limits of Shariah. Whoever disobeys Allah out of fear of creation has feared other than Allah. If he refrains from disobedience due to fear of creation and observes the limits of Shariah, he fears none but Allah.

### PLANNED REVISION

A student of knowledge should set a specific plan for themselves in terms of revision and repetition. The heart does not settle until it reaches the desired level of mastery.

It is recommended to revise the lesson from the previous day five times, the lesson from two days prior four times, the one from three days prior three times, and so on, reducing the repetitions incrementally. This method ensures better retention and mastery. The student should avoid repeating lessons silently because studying and revising should be done with energy and vigour. However, one should not raise one's voice so loudly that it becomes exhausting, preventing one from continuing one's repetition. The best course of action is moderation, as "the best of matters is the balanced one."

It is narrated that Abū Yūsuf ﵀ would discuss jurisprudence with scholars with great strength and enthusiasm. His son-in-law, observing him, remarked in amazement: "I know he has not eaten for five days, yet he debates with such energy and liveliness."

---

(7) Translator: I did not find the Hadith in this wording, rather with these words: استعيذوا بالله من طمع يهدي إلى طبع ومن طمع في غير مطمع حين لا مطمع ("Seek refuge in Allah from greed that leads to disgraceful behaviour and from desiring what is unattainable when there is no hope for it."). The narration attributed to Mu'ādh ibn Jabal, as documented in *Takhrīj al-Musnad* by Shu'ayb al-Arnā'ut (Hadith no. 22021), has been classified by the *muḥaddith* as having a weak chain of transmission (*isnād da'īf*).

يُدْنِي إِلَى طَبَعٍ». وَيَنْبَغِي لِلْمُؤْمِنِ أَلَّا يَرْجُو إِلَّا مِنَ اللهِ تَعَالَىٰ، وَلَا يَخَافُ إِلَّا مِنْهُ، وَيَظْهَرُ ذَلِكَ بِمُجَاوَزَةِ حَدِّ الشَّرْعِ وَعَدَمِهَا، فَمَنْ عَصَى اللَّهَ تَعَالَىٰ خَوْفًا مِنَ الْمَخْلُوقِ فَقَدْ خَافَ غَيْرَ اللَّهِ، فَإِذَا لَمْ يَعْصِ اللَّهَ تَعَالَىٰ لِخَوْفِ الْمَخْلُوقِ وَرَاقَبَ حُدُودَ الشَّرْعِ، فَلَمْ يَخَفْ غَيْرَ اللَّهِ تَعَالَىٰ؛ بَلْ خَافَ اللَّهَ تَعَالَىٰ، وَكَذَا فِي جَانِبِ الرَّجَاءِ.

وَيَنْبَغِي لِطَالِبِ الْعِلْمِ أَنْ يَعِدَّ وَيُقَدِّرَ لِنَفْسِهِ تَقْدِيرًا فِي التَّكْرَارِ؛ فَإِنَّهُ لَا يَسْتَقِرُّ قَلْبُهُ حَتَّى يَبْلُغَ ذَلِكَ الْمَبْلَغَ.

وَيَنْبَغِي أَنْ يُكَرِّرَ سَبَقَ الْأَمْسِ خَمْسَ مَرَّاتٍ، وَسَبَقَ الْيَوْمِ الَّذِي قَبْلَ الْأَمْسِ أَرْبَعَ مَرَّاتٍ، وَالسَّبَقَ الَّذِي قَبْلَهُ ثَلَاثًا، وَالَّذِي قَبْلَهُ اثْنَيْنِ، وَالَّذِي قَبْلَهُ وَاحِدًا، فَهَذَا أَدْعَىٰ إِلَى الْحِفْظِ وَالتَّكْرَارِ.

وَيَنْبَغِي أَلَّا يَعْتَادَ الْمُخَافَتَةَ فِي التَّكْرَارِ؛ لِأَنَّ الدَّرْسَ وَالتَّكْرَارَ يَنْبَغِي أَنْ يَكُونَ بِقُوَّةٍ وَنَشَاطٍ، وَلَا يَجْهَرَ جَهْرًا يُجْهِدُ نَفْسَهُ كَيْلَا يَنْقَطِعَ عَنِ التَّكْرَارِ، فَـ «خَيْرُ الْأُمُورِ أَوْسَطُهَا».

وَحُكِيَ أَنَّ أَبَا يُوسُفَ رَحِمَهُ اللهُ كَانَ يُذَاكِرُ الْفِقْهَ مَعَ الْفُقَهَاءِ بِقُوَّةٍ وَنَشَاطٍ، وَكَانَ صِهْرُهُ عِنْدَهُ يَتَعَجَّبُ فِي أَمْرِهِ يَقُولُ: أَنَا أَعْلَمُ أَنَّهُ جَائِعٌ مُذْ خَمْسَةِ أَيَّامٍ، وَمَعَ ذَلِكَ يُنَاظِرُ بِقُوَّةٍ وَنَشَاطٍ.

## PERSEVERANCE IN STUDY

A student should avoid periods of inactivity, as these are detrimental. Shaykh al-Islām Burhān al-Dīn ﷺ said: "I excelled over my peers because I never experienced a period of inactivity in my studies."

It was narrated about Shaykh al-Isbijābī that during his time of seeking knowledge and studying, he experienced a period of stagnation lasting twelve years due to a political upheaval and the overturning of the ruling authority.

Along with his study partner, he left their location to a place where they could continue their pursuit of knowledge. Despite the challenges, they remained steadfast in their studies and never abandoned their daily sessions of debate and mutual learning. For twelve consecutive years, they consistently engaged in these debates without interruption.

As a result of their dedication, his study partner became the Shaykh al-Islām for the Shāfiʿīs, and Shaykh al-Isbijābī himself adhered to the Shāfiʿī school of jurisprudence.

Our teacher, al-Qāḍī al-Imām Fakhr al-Islām, Qāḍī Khān used to say: "It is necessary for a student of jurisprudence (*mutafaqqih*) to memorise one book from among the books of jurisprudence consistently. This will make it easier for him, thereafter, to retain what he hears from the field of jurisprudence."

وَيَنْبَغِي أَلَّا يَكُونَ لِطَالِبِ الْعِلْمِ فَتْرَةٌ، فَإِنَّهَا آفَةٌ، وَكَانَ أُسْتَاذُنَا شَيْخُ الْإِسْلَامِ بُرْهَانُ الدِّينِ رَحِمَهُ اللهُ يَقُولُ: إِنَّمَا غَلَبْتُ شُرَكَائِي بِأَنِّي لَمْ تَقَعْ لِي الْفَتْرَةُ فِي التَّحْصِيلِ.

وَكَانَ يَحْكِي عَنِ الشَّيْخِ الْإِسْبِيجَابِيِّ أَنَّهُ وَقَعَ فِي زَمَانِ تَحْصِيلِهِ وَتَعَلُّمِهِ فَتْرَةَ اثْنَتَيْ عَشْرَةَ سَنَةً بِانْقِلَابِ الْمُلْكِ، فَخَرَجَ مَعَ شَرِيكِهِ فِي الْمُنَاظَرَةِ [إِلَى حَيْثُ يُمْكِنُهُمَا الاسْتِمْرَارُ فِي طَلَبِ الْعِلْمِ وَظَلَّا يَدْرُسَانِهِ مَعًا] وَلَمْ يَتْرُكَا الْمُنَاظَرَةَ وَكَانَا يَجْلِسَانِ فِي الْمُنَاظَرَةِ كُلَّ يَوْمٍ، وَلَمْ يَتْرُكَا الْجُلُوسَ لِلْمُنَاظَرَةِ اثْنَتَيْ عَشْرَةَ سَنَةً. فَصَارَ شَرِيكُهُ شَيْخَ الْإِسْلَامِ لِلشَّافِعِيِّينَ وَكَانَ هُوَ شَافِعِيًّا.

وَكَانَ أُسْتَاذُنَا الشَّيْخُ الْقَاضِي الْإِمَامُ فَخْرُ الْإِسْلَامِ قَاضِي خَانْ يَقُولُ: يَنْبَغِي لِلْمُتَفَقِّهِ أَنْ يَحْفَظَ [كِتَابًا] وَاحِدًا مِنْ [كُتُبِ] الْفِقْهِ دَائِمًا، فَيَتَيَسَّرُ لَهُ بَعْدَ ذَلِكَ حِفْظُ مَا سَمِعَ مِنَ الْفِقْهِ.

It is essential for a seeker of knowledge (*ṭālib al-ʿilm*) to rely upon Allah in his pursuit of knowledge and not to concern himself excessively about sustenance. His heart should not be preoccupied with such matters.

Abū Ḥanīfah ﷺ narrated from ʿAbdullāh ibn al-Ḥārith al-Zubaydī, a companion of the Messenger of Allah ﷺ: "Whoever devotes themselves to understanding the religion of Allah, Allah will relieve their worries and provide for them from sources they do not anticipate."

Indeed, those who fill their hearts with concerns about sustenance – whether food or clothing – rarely find the time to cultivate noble manners and pursue lofty aims.

It is said:

*Forsake lofty ambitions; do not strive to achieve them,*
*Sit content, for you are the one who eats and dresses.*

A man once said to Ibn Manṣūr al-Ḥallāj: "Advise me." He replied: "It is your soul – if you do not occupy it, it will occupy you."

Thus, everyone should engage themselves in virtuous deeds so that their desires do not preoccupy them. A wise person does not concern himself excessively with worldly matters, for worry and sorrow neither reverse calamities nor bring benefit. Instead, they harm the heart, body, and mind, and disrupt virtuous deeds. He has concern for the Hereafter because it is beneficial.

As for the statement of the Prophet ﷺ: "Among sins are those that cannot be expiated except by the worry of livelihood", this refers to a moderate degree of concern that does not disrupt virtuous deeds or excessively preoccupy the heart, impeding focus during prayer. Such moderate concern and intention are themselves acts of devotion.

## فصل: فِي التَّوَكُّلِ

ثُمَّ لَا بُدَّ لِطَالِبِ الْعِلْمِ مِنَ التَّوَكُّلِ فِي طَلَبِ الْعِلْمِ وَلَا يَهْتَمَّ لِأَمْرِ الرِّزْقِ، وَلَا يُشْغِلَ قَلْبَهُ بِذَلِكَ.

رَوَى أَبُو حَنِيفَةَ رَحِمَهُ اللَّهُ عَنْ عَبْدِ اللهِ بْنِ الْحَارِثِ الزَّبِيدِيِّ صَاحِبِ رَسُولِ اللَّهِ ﷺ: «مَنْ تَفَقَّهَ فِي دِينِ اللَّهِ كَفِيَ هَمَّهُ اللَّهُ تَعَالَى وَرَزَقَهُ مِنْ حَيْثُ لَا يَحْتَسِبُ»، فَإِنَّ مَنِ اشْتَغَلَ قَلْبُهُ بِأَمْرِ الرِّزْقِ مِنَ الْقُوتِ وَالْكِسْوَةِ قَلَّمَا يَتَفَرَّغُ لِتَحْصِيلِ مَكَارِمِ الْأَخْلَاقِ وَمَعَالِي الْأُمُورِ.

قِيلَ:

دَعِ الْمَكَارِمَ لَا تَرْحَلْ لِبُغْيَتِهَا ... وَاقْعُدْ فَإِنَّكَ أَنْتَ الطَّاعِمُ الْكَاسِي

قَالَ رَجُلٌ لِابْنِ مَنْصُورٍ الْحَلَّاجِ: أَوْصِنِي، فَقَالَ ابْنُ مَنْصُورٍ: هِيَ نَفْسُكَ، إِنْ لَمْ تَشْغَلْهَا شَغَلَتْكَ.

فَيَنْبَغِي لِكُلِّ أَحَدٍ أَنْ يُشْغِلَ نَفْسَهُ بِأَعْمَالِ الْخَيْرِ حَتَّى لَا يُشْغِلَ نَفْسَهُ بِهَوَاهَا، وَلَا يَهْتَمُّ الْعَاقِلُ لِأَمْرِ الدُّنْيَا؛ لِأَنَّ الْهَمَّ وَالْحُزْنَ لَا يَرُدُّ الْمُصِيبَةَ وَلَا يَنْفَعُ بَلْ يَضُرُّ بِالْقَلْبِ وَالْبَدَنِ وَالْعَقْلِ، وَيُخِلُّ بِأَعْمَالِ الْخَيْرِ، وَيَهْتَمُّ لِأَمْرِ الْآخِرَةِ لِأَنَّهُ يَنْفَعُ.

وَأَمَّا قَوْلُهُ عَلَيْهِ الصَّلَاةُ وَالسَّلَامُ: «إِنَّ مِنَ الذُّنُوبِ ذُنُوبًا لَا يُكَفِّرُهَا إِلَّا هَمُّ الْمَعِيشَةِ»، فَالْمُرَادُ مِنْهُ قَدْرُ هَمٍّ لَا يُخِلُّ بِأَعْمَالِ الْخَيْرِ، وَلَا يُشْغِلُ الْقَلْبَ شُغْلًا يُخِلُّ بِإِحْضَارِ الْقَلْبِ فِي الصَّلَاةِ، فَإِنَّ ذَلِكَ الْقَدْرَ مِنَ الْهَمِّ وَالْقَصْدِ مِنْ أَعْمَالِ الْآخِرَةِ.

A seeker of knowledge must minimise worldly attachments as much as possible. For this reason, estrangement (*ghurbah*) was often preferred by scholars.

Additionally, a student must endure hardships and difficulties in the journey of learning. As Mūsā ﷺ said during his journey for knowledge: "We have certainly suffered in this journey of ours much fatigue" (*al-Kahf*, 62). This was not reported for any of his other travels, indicating that the pursuit of knowledge inherently involves hardship. This is because seeking knowledge is a great endeavour and, according to most scholars, surpasses engaging in jihad.

The reward is commensurate with the effort and toil; those who persevere through such challenges will experience the sweetness of knowledge, which surpasses all other worldly pleasures. Muhammad ibn al-Ḥasan ﷺ would say after sleepless nights resolving complex issues: "Where are the children of kings from these pleasures?"

### CONSTANT ENGAGEMENT WITH KNOWLEDGE

A student of knowledge should not be preoccupied with anything other than his studies and should not turn away from jurisprudence (*fiqh*).

Muhammad ibn al-Ḥasan ﷺ said: "Our profession is from the cradle to the grave. Whoever wishes to leave it even for an hour may do so – but only for that hour."

It is narrated that Ibrāhīm ibn al-Jarrāḥ, a jurist, visited Abū Yūsuf during his final illness. As Abū Yūsuf was in the throes of death, he asked: "Is stoning the Jamarāt while riding better or on foot?" When Ibrāhīm could not answer, Abū Yūsuf himself provided the answer. Thus, a jurist should remain engaged in his studies at all times. In this lies immense joy and fulfilment.

It is said that Muhammad ibn al-Ḥasan was seen in a dream after his death. When asked: "How did you find the moment

وَلَا بُدَّ لِطَالِبِ الْعِلْمِ مِنْ تَقْلِيلِ الْعَلَائِقِ الدُّنْيَوِيَّةِ بِقَدْرِ الْوُسْعِ؛ فَلِهَذَا اخْتَارُوا الْغُرْبَةَ.

وَلَا بُدَّ لِطَالِبِ الْعِلْمِ مِنْ تَحَمُّلِ النَّصَبِ وَالْمَشَقَّةِ فِي سَفَرِ التَّعَلُّمِ، كَمَا قَالَ مُوسَى - صَلَوَاتُ اللَّهِ عَلَىٰ نَبِيِّنَا وَعَلَيْهِ- فِي سَفَرِ التَّعَلُّمِ وَلَمْ يُنْقَلْ عَنْهُ ذَلِكَ فِي غَيْرِهِ مِنَ الْأَسْفَارِ: ﴿لَقَدْ لَقِينَا مِن سَفَرِنَا هَذَا نَصَبًا﴾ [الكهف]؛ لِيُعْلَمَ أَنَّ سَفَرَ الْعِلْمِ لَا يَخْلُو عَنِ التَّعَبِ؛ لِأَنَّ طَلَبَ الْعِلْمِ أَمْرٌ عَظِيمٌ وَهُوَ أَفْضَلُ مِنَ الْغُزَاةِ عِنْدَ أَكْثَرِ الْعُلَمَاءِ، وَالْأَجْرُ عَلَىٰ قَدْرِ التَّعَبِ وَالنَّصَبِ، فَمَنْ صَبَرَ عَلَىٰ ذَلِكَ التَّعَبِ وَجَدَ لَذَّةَ الْعِلْمِ تَفُوقُ سَائِرَ لَذَّاتِ الدُّنْيَا.

وَلِهَذَا كَانَ مُحَمَّدُ بْنُ الْحَسَنِ -إِذَا سَهِرَ اللَّيَالِي وَانْحَلَّتْ لَهُ الْمُشْكِلَاتُ- يَقُولُ: أَيْنَ أَبْنَاءُ الْمُلُوكِ مِنْ هَذِهِ اللَّذَّاتِ؟

وَيَنْبَغِي لِطَالِبِ الْعِلْمِ أَلَّا يَشْتَغِلَ بِشَيْءٍ آخَرَ غَيْرِ الْعِلْمِ وَلَا يُعْرِضَ عَنِ الْفِقْهِ.

قَالَ مُحَمَّدُ بْنُ الْحَسَنِ رَحِمَهُ اللَّهُ: صِنَاعَتُنَا هَذِهِ مِنَ الْمَهْدِ إِلَى اللَّحْدِ، فَمَنْ أَرَادَ أَنْ يَتْرُكَ عِلْمَنَا هذا سَاعَةً؛ فَلْيَتْرُكْهُ السَّاعَةَ.

وَدَخَلَ فَقِيهٌ - وَهُوَ إِبْرَاهِيمُ بْنُ الْجَرَّاحِ -، عَلَىٰ أَبِي يُوسُفَ يَعُودُهُ فِي مَرَضِ مَوْتِهِ وَهُوَ يَجُودُ بِنَفْسِهِ، فَقَالَ أَبُو يُوسُفَ: رَمْيُ الْجِمَارِ رَاكِبًا أَفْضَلُ أَمْ رَاجِلًا؟ فَلَمْ يَعْرِفِ الْجَوَابَ، فَأَجَابَ بِنَفْسِهِ.

of death?" he replied: "I was contemplating an issue of *mukātabah*[8], and I did not even notice the departure of my soul."

It is also narrated that he remarked at the end of his life: "The issues of *mukātabah* preoccupied me from preparing for this day", though he likely said this out of humility.

(8) In Islamic law, الْمُكَاتَب (*al-mukātab*) refers to a slave who has entered into a written contract (*kitāba*) with his master to purchase his freedom. The contract stipulates that the slave will pay a specified amount of money, either in a lump sum or installments, after which he will become free.

وَهَكَذَا يَنْبَغِي لِلْفَقِيهِ أَنْ يَشْتَغِلَ بِهِ فِي جَمِيعِ أَوْقَاتِهِ فَحِينَئِذٍ يَجِدُ لَذَّةً عَظِيمَةً فِي ذَلِكَ.

وَقِيلَ : رُئِيَ مُحَمَّدُ [بْنُ الْحَسَنِ] فِي الْمَنَامِ بَعْدَ وَفَاتِهِ، فَقِيلَ لَهُ: كَيْفَ كُنْتَ فِي حَالِ النَّزْعِ؟ فَقَالَ: كُنْتُ مُتَأَمِّلًا فِي مَسْأَلَةٍ مِنْ مَسَائِلِ الْمُكَاتَبِ، فَلَمْ أَشْعُرْ بِخُرُوجِ رُوحِي.

وَقِيلَ : إِنَّهُ قَالَ فِي آخِرِ عُمُرِهِ: شَغَلَتْنِي مَسَائِلُ الْمُكَاتَبِ عَنِ الِاسْتِعْدَادِ لِهَذَا الْيَوْمِ، وَإِنَّمَا قَالَ ذَلِكَ تَوَاضُعًا.

It is said: "The time for learning extends from the cradle to the grave."

Ḥasan ibn Ziyād began studying jurisprudence (*fiqh*) at the age of eighty. He refrained from sleeping on a bed for forty years and then issued legal rulings for another forty years.

The best times for study are during one's youth, in the pre-dawn hours (*saḥar*), and between the prayers of *maghrib* and *ʿishāʾ* (*al-ʿishāʾayn*).

One should dedicate all one's time to learning, and if one tires of one subject, one should turn to another. Ibn ʿAbbās ﷺ would say when weary of discourse: "Bring me the collection of poetry." Muhammad ibn al-Ḥasan would stay awake at night with books beside him. When he grew tired of one subject, he would turn to another. He kept water nearby to remove drowsiness, saying: "Sleep results from excess heat."

# فصل: فِي وَقْتِ التَّحْصِيلِ

قِيلَ: وَقْتُ التَّعَلُّمِ مِنَ الْمَهْدِ إِلَى اللَّحْدِ.

دَخَلَ حَسَنُ بْنُ زِيَادٍ فِي التَّفَقُّهِ، وَهُوَ ابْنُ ثَمَانِينَ سَنَةً، وَلَمْ يَبِتْ عَلَى الْفِرَاشِ أَرْبَعِينَ سَنَةً، فَأَفْتَىٰ بَعْدَ ذَلِكَ أَرْبَعِينَ سَنَةً.

وَأَفْضَلُ الْأَوْقَاتِ شَرْخُ الشَّبَابِ، وَوَقْتُ السَّحَرِ، وَمَا بَيْنَ الْعِشَاءَيْنِ.

وَيَنْبَغِي أَنْ يَسْتَغْرِقَ جَمِيعَ أَوْقَاتِهِ، فَإِذَا مَلَّ مِنْ عِلْمٍ يَشْتَغِلُ بِعِلْمٍ آخَرَ.

وَكَانَ ابْنُ عَبَاسٍ رَضِيَ اللَّهُ عَنْهُ إِذَا مَلَّ مِنَ الْكَلَامِ يَقُولُ: هَاتُوا دِيوَانَ الشُّعَرَاءِ. وَكَانَ مُحَمَّدُ بْنُ الْحَسَنِ لَا يَنَامُ اللَّيْلَ، وَكَانَ يَضَعُ عِنْدَهُ الدَّفَاتِرَ، وَكَانَ إِذَا مَلَّ مِنْ نَوْعٍ يَنْظُرُ فِي نَوْعٍ آخَرَ، وَكَانَ يَضَعُ عِنْدَهُ الْمَاءَ، وَيُزِيلَ نَوْمَهُ بِالْمَاءِ، وَكَانَ يَقُولُ: إِنَّ النَّوْمَ مِنَ الْحَرَارَةِ.

A scholar should be compassionate and sincere, not envious, for envy harms but does not benefit. Our teacher, Shaykh al-Islām, Burhān al-Dīn ﷺ said: "It is said that the son of a teacher often becomes a scholar because the teacher wishes for his student to excel in the Qurʾan. By the blessings of such intent and compassion, his son becomes learned."

Abū al-Ḥasan narrated that al-Ṣadr al-Ajall Burhān al-Aʾimmah assigned study times for his two sons, al-Ṣadr al-Shahīd Ḥusām al-Dīn and al-Ṣadr al-Saʿīd Tāj al-Dīn, during the late morning (*al-ḍaḥwah al-kubrāʾ*), after attending to all other students. When his sons remarked that they often grew tired during that time, he replied: "Foreign students and the children of dignitaries come to me from distant lands, so I must prioritise their lessons." By the blessings of his compassion, his sons surpassed most jurists of their time in their respective regions.

One should not engage in disputes or arguments, as they waste valuable time.

It is said: "The benefactor will be rewarded for his kindness, and the wrongdoer will be sufficed by his misdeeds." Shaykh al-Imām Rukn al-Islām Muhammad ibn Abī Bakr ﷺ, known as Imām Khawāhir Zādah, the mufti of the two groups, narrated to me from the Sulṭān of Tarīqah and Sharīʿah Yūsuf al-Hamadānī:

*Let the wrongdoer be; do not repay his evil.*
*His own deeds will suffice to deal with him.*

It is also said: "Whoever wishes to humble his enemy should focus on self-improvement."

A poet remarked:

*If you wish to see your enemy humiliated,*
*Burdened with grief and overwhelmed by anxiety,*

## فصل فِي الشَّفَقَةِ وَالنَّصِيحَةِ

يَنْبَغِي أَنْ يَكُونَ صَاحِبُ الْعِلْمِ مُشْفِقًا نَاصِحًا غَيْرَ حَاسِدٍ، فَالْحَسَدُ يَضُرُّ وَلَا يَنْفَعُ. وَكَانَ أُسْتَاذُنَا شَيْخُ الْإِسْلَامِ بُرْهَانُ الدِّينِ رَحِمَهُ اللهُ يَقُولُ: قَالُوا إِنَّ ابْنَ الْمُعَلِّمِ يَكُونُ عَالِمًا؛ لِأَنَّ الْمُعَلِّمَ يُرِيدُ أَنْ يَكُونَ تِلْمِيذُهُ فِي الْقُرْآنِ عَالِمًا فَبِبَرَكَةِ اعْتِقَادِهِ وَشَفَقَتِهِ يَكُونُ ابْنُهُ عَالِمًا.

وَكَانَ أَبُو الْحَسَنِ يَحْكِي أَنَّ الصَّدْرَ الْأَجَلَّ بُرْهَانُ الْأَئِمَّةِ جعَلَ وَقْتَ السَّبْقِ لِابْنَيْهِ الصَّدْرِ الشَّهِيدِ حُسَامِ الدِّينِ، وَالصَّدْرِ السَّعِيدِ تَاجِ الدِّينِ وَقْتَ الضَّحْوَةِ الْكُبْرَىٰ بَعْدَ جَمِيعِ الْأَسْبَاقِ، وَكَانَا يَقُولَانِ: إِنَّ طَبِيعَتَنَا تَكِلُّ وَتَمَلُّ فِي ذَلِكَ الْوَقْتِ، فَقَالَ أَبُوهُمَا رَحِمَهُ اللهُ: إِنَّ الْغُرَبَاءَ وَأَوْلَادَ الْكُبَرَاءِ، يَأْتُونَنِي مِنْ أَقْطَارِ الْأَرْضِ فَلَا بُدَّ مِنْ أَنْ أُقَدِّمَ أَسْبَاقَهُمْ. فَبِبَرَكَةِ شَفَقَتِهِ فَاقَ ابْنَاهُ عَلَىٰ أَكْثَرِ فُقَهَاءِ الْأَمْصَارِ، وَأَهْلَ الْأَرْضِ فِي ذَلِكَ الْعَصْرِ.

وَيَنْبَغِي أَلَّا يُنَازِعَ أَحَدًا وَلَا يُخَاصِمَهُ؛ لِأَنَّهُ يُضَيِّعُ أَوْقَاتَهُ.

قِيلَ: الْمُحْسِنُ سَيُجْزَىٰ بِإِحْسَانِهِ، وَالْمُسِيءُ سَتَكْفِيهِ مَسَاوِيهِ.

أَنْشَدَنِي الشَّيْخُ الْإِمَامُ الزَّاهِدُ الْعَارِفُ رُكْنُ الْإِسْلَامِ مُحَمَّدُ بْنُ أَبِي بِكْرِ الْمَعْرُوفُ بِإِمَامِ خَوَاهِرْ زَادَهْ مُفْتِي الْفَرِيقَيْنِ رَحِمَهُ اللهُ: قَالَ: أَنْشَدَنِي سُلْطَانُ الشَّرِيعَةِ وَالطَّرِيقَةِ يُوسُفُ الهَمَذَانِيُّ:

دَعِ الْمَرْءَ لَا تَجْزِهْ عَلَىٰ سُوءِ فِعْلِهِ     سَيَكْفِيهِ مَا فِيهِ وَمَا هُوَ فَاعِلُهْ

قِيلَ: مَنْ أَرَادَ أَنْ يُرْغِمَ أَنْفَ عَدُوِّهِ فَلْيُكَرِّرْ.

*Strive for greatness and increase your knowledge,*
*For with every gain in knowledge, your enemy's envy will grow.*

It is said: "Focus on benefiting yourself rather than overpowering your enemy. If you attend to your own well-being and interests, that will, in turn, overpower your enemy. Avoid enmity, for it exposes your weaknesses and wastes your time. Instead, turn away from conflict, especially with the ignorant." Jesus, son of Mary, ﷺ said: "Bear one act of foolishness from a fool and you will gain tenfold in reward."

Someone recited the following lines of poetry:

*I tested people, century after century,*
*And found none but deceivers and those who harbour hatred.*
*In times of calamity, nothing strikes harder,*
*And no burden is heavier than the enmity of men.*
*I tasted the bitterness of all things,*
*But nothing was more bitter than asking for favours.*

### AVOIDING SUSPICION AND CONFLICT

Avoid suspicion towards believers, for suspicion is the root of enmity and is impermissible. The Prophet ﷺ said: "Think well of the believers." Suspicion arises from a corrupt nature and an impure heart. Just as Abū al-Ṭayyib said:

*When a man's deeds are vile, his suspicions worsen,*
*And he trusts what his imagination contrives.*
*He turns against his allies, believing his enemies,*
*And becomes lost in a night of doubtful gloom.*

Someone recited to me:

*Avoid the vile, do not engage with them,*
*And increase kindness towards those you've blessed.*
*Your enemies' schemes will fail to harm you,*
*For if they plot, you should not do the same.*

Al-ʿAmīd Abū al-Fatḥ al-Bustī recited to me:

وَأُنْشِدْتُ هذا الشِّعْرَ:

إِذَا شِئْتَ أَنْ تَلْقَىٰ عَدُوَّكَ رَاغِمًا وَتَقْتُلَهُ غَمًّا وَتُحْرِقَهُ هَمًّا
فَرُمْ لِلْعُلَىٰ وَازْدَدْ مِنَ الْعِلْمِ إِنَّهُ مَنِ ازْدَادَ عِلْمًا زَادَ حَاسِدُهُ غَمًّا

قِيلَ: عَلَيْكَ أَنْ تَشْتَغِلَ بِمَصَالِحِ نَفْسِكَ لَا بِقَهْرِ عَدُوِّكَ، فَإِذَا أَقَمْتَ مَصَالِحَ نَفْسِكَ تَضَمَّنَ ذَلِكَ قَهْرَ عَدُوِّكَ، وَإِيَّاكَ وَالْمُعَادَاةَ فَإِنَّهَا تَفْضَحُكَ وَتُضَيِّعُ أَوْقَاتَكَ، وَعَلَيْكَ بِالتَّحَوُّلِ لَا سِيَّمَا مِنَ السُّفَهَاءِ.
قَالَ عِيسَى ابْنُ مَرْيَمَ - صَلَوَاتُ اللهِ عَلَيْهِ -: احْتَمِلُوا مِنَ السَّفِيهِ وَاحِدَةً كَيْ تَرْبَحُوا عَشْرًا.
وَأُنْشِدْتُ لِبَعْضِهِمْ:

بَلَوْتُ النَّاسَ قَرْنًا بَعْدَ قَرْنٍ وَلَمْ أَرَ غَيْرَ خَتَّالٍ وَقَالِي
وَلَمْ أَرَ فِي الْخُطُوبِ أَشَدَّ وَقْعًا وَأَصْعَبَ مِنْ مُعَادَاةِ الرِّجَالِ
وَذُقْتُ مَرَارَةَ الْأَشْيَاءِ طُرًّا وَمَا ذُقْتُ أَمَرَّ مِنَ السُّؤَالِ

وَإِيَّاكَ أَنْ تَظُنَّ بِالْمُؤْمِنِ سُوءًا، فَإِنَّهُ مَنْشَأُ الْعَدَاوَةِ، وَلَا يَحِلُّ ذَلِكَ، لِقَوْلِهِ عَلَيْهِ الصَّلَاةُ وَالسَّلَامُ: «ظُنُّوا بِالْمُؤْمِنِينَ خَيْرًا»، وَإِنَّمَا يَنْشَأُ ذَلِكَ مِنْ خُبْثِ النِّيَّةِ وَسُوءِ السَّرِيرَةِ، كَمَا قَالَ أَبُو الطَّيِّبِ:

إِذَا سَاءَ فِعْلُ الْمَرْءِ سَاءَتْ ظُنُونُهُ وَصَدَّقَ مَا يَعْتَادُهُ مِنْ تَوَهُّمِ
وَعَادَى مُحِبِّيهِ بِقَوْلِ عُدَاتِهِ وَأَصْبَحَ فِي لَيْلٍ مِنَ الشَّكِّ مُظْلِمِ

*A wise man will never be safe from an ignorant person,*
*Who oppresses him with injustice and burdens him with hardship.*
*So choose peace over conflict with such individuals,*
*And let patience and silence be your armour.*

وَأُنْشِدْتُ لِبَعْضِهِمْ:

تَنَحَّ عَنِ الْقَبِيحِ وَلَا تَرِدْهُ    وَمَنْ أَوْلَيْتَهُ حُسْنًا فَزِدْهُ
سَتُكْفِي مِنْ عَدُوِّكَ كُلَّ كَيْدٍ    إِذَا كَادَ الْعَدُوُّ فَلَا تَكِدْهُ

وَأُنْشِدَتُ لِلشَّيْخِ الْعَمِيدِ أَبِي الْفَتْحِ الْبُسْتِيِّ:

ذُو الْعَقْلِ لَا يَسْلَمُ مِنْ جَاهِلٍ    يَسُومُهُ ظُلْمًا وَإِعْنَاتًا
فَلْيَخْتَرِ السِّلْمَ عَلَى حَرْبِهِ    وَلْيُلْزِمِ الْإِنْصَاتَ إِنْصَاتًا

A student of knowledge (*ṭālib al-ʿilm*) should continuously seek benefit at all times so that he may achieve excellence and completeness in knowledge. The method of deriving benefit is to always carry an inkwell (*miḥbarah*) so he can record the insights he hears from scholars and intellectuals.

It is said: "Whoever memorises escapes, and whoever writes preserves." It is also said: "True knowledge is what is taken from the mouths of men, for they retain the best of what they hear and share the best of what they preserve." I heard al-Imām al-Adīb al-Ustādh Zayn al-Islām, known as al-Adīb al-Mukhtār, narrate: Hilāl ibn Zayd ibn Yasār said: "I saw the Prophet ﷺ speaking to his companions about knowledge and wisdom. I said, 'O Messenger of Allah, repeat for me what you said to them.' He asked: 'Do you have an inkwell with you?' I replied: 'I do not.' The Prophet ﷺ said: 'O Hilāl, do not part with an inkwell, for there is goodness in it and in its people until the Day of Judgement.'"

Al-Ṣadr al-Shahīd Ḥusām al-Dīn advised his son Shams al-Dīn: "Memorise something from knowledge and wisdom daily. Even if it seems little, over time it will become abundant."

ʿIṣām ibn Yūsuf purchased a pen for a dinar to record what he learned immediately, saying: "Life is short, and knowledge is vast." A student of knowledge should not waste time and hours but seize the nights and moments of solitude.

It is narrated that Yaḥyā ibn Muʿādh al-Rāzī said: "The night is long, so do not shorten it with sleep, And the day is bright, so do not darken it with sins."

A student should take advantage of his teachers and learn from them, as not everything missed can be regained. Shaykh al-Islām once remarked in his *Mashyakha*: "How many great scholars did I encounter, yet I failed to ask them questions!"

Reflecting on this regret, I composed the following lines:

# فصل في الاسْتِفَادَةِ وَاقْتِبَاسِ الْأَدَبِ

وَيَنْبَغِي أَنْ يَكُونَ طَالِبُ الْعِلْمِ مُسْتَفِيدًا فِي كُلِّ وَقْتٍ حَتَّىٰ يَحْصُلَ لَهُ الْفَضْلُ وَالْكَمَالُ فِي الْعِلْمِ، وَطَرِيقُ الاسْتِفَادَةِ أَنْ يَكُونَ مَعَهُ فِي كُلِّ وَقْتٍ مِحْبَرَةٌ حَتَّىٰ يَكْتُبَ مَا يَسْمَعُ مِنَ الْفَوَائِدِ الْعِلْمِيَّةِ.

قِيلَ: مَنْ حَفِظَ فَرَّ وَمَنْ كَتَبَ قَرَّ.

وَقِيلَ: الْعِلْمُ مَا يُؤْخَذُ مِنْ أَفْوَاهِ الرِّجَالِ؛ لِأَنَّهُمْ يَحْفَظُونَ أَحْسَنَ مَا يَسْمَعُونَ، وَيَقُولُونَ أَحْسَنَ مَا يَحْفَظُونَ.

وَسَمِعْتُ عَنِ الشَّيْخِ الْإِمَامِ الْأَدِيبِ الْأُسْتَاذِ زَيْنِ الْإِسْلَامِ الْمَعْرُوفِ بِالْأَدِيبِ الْمُخْتَارِ يَقُولُ: قَالَ هِلَالُ [ابْنُ زَيْدِ] بْنِ يَسَارٍ: رَأَيْتُ النَّبِيَّ ﷺ يَقُولُ لِأَصْحَابِهِ شَيْئًا مِنَ الْعِلْمِ وَالْحِكْمَةِ، فَقُلْتُ: يَا رَسُولَ اللَّهِ؛ أَعِدْ لِي مَا قُلْتَ لَهُمْ، فَقَالَ لِي: هَلْ مَعَكَ مِحْبَرَةٌ؟» فَقُلْتُ: مَا مَعِي مِحْبَرَةٌ، فَقَالَ النَّبِيُّ عَلَيْهِ السَّلَامُ: يَا هِلَالُ، لَا تُفَارِقِ الْمِحْبَرَةَ، فَإِنَّ الْخَيْرَ فِيهَا وَفِي أَهْلِهَا إِلَىٰ يَوْمِ الْقِيَامَةِ».

وَوَصَى الصَّدْرُ الشَّهِيدُ حُسَامُ الدِّينِ ابْنَهُ شَمْسَ الدِّينِ أَنْ يَحْفَظَ كُلَّ يَوْمٍ شَيْئًا مِنَ الْعِلْمِ وَالْحِكْمَةِ فَإِنَّه يَسِيرٌ، وَعَنْ قَرِيبٍ يَكُونُ كَثِيرًا.

وَاشْتَرَىٰ عِصَامُ بْنُ يُوسُفَ قَلَمًا بِدِينَارٍ لِيَكْتُبَ مَا يَسْمَعُهُ فِي الْحَالِ، فَالْعُمْرُ قَصِيرٌ وَالْعِلْمُ كَثِيرٌ.

فَيَنْبَغِي أَلَّا يُضَيِّعَ طَالِبُ الْعِلْمِ الْأَوْقَاتَ وَالسَّاعَاتِ وَيَغْتَنِمَ اللَّيَالِي وَالْخَلَوَاتِ.

*Alas for the loss of such meetings, alas!*
*Not everything that is lost or fades can be found.*

ʿAlī ibn Abī Ṭālib (may Allah ennoble his face) said: "When you engage in something, dedicate yourself fully to it." Neglecting the pursuit of knowledge is a disgrace and a loss. A student should seek refuge in Allah, day and night, from such neglect.

A student of knowledge must endure hardship and humility in the pursuit of learning. Flattery is generally condemned, except in the context of seeking knowledge, where it becomes necessary – whether towards a teacher, a peer, or others – from whom one might benefit. It is said: Knowledge is an honour that carries no disgrace, but it cannot be attained except through an effort that has no glory.

As another put it:

*I see you desire to honour yourself,*
*But you shall not gain honour until you humble it.*

يُحكَى عَنْ يَحيَى بْنِ مُعَاذٍ الرَّازِيّ [أَنَّهُ قَالَ:] اللَّيْلُ طَوِيلٌ فَلاَ تُقَصِّرْهُ بِمَنَامِكَ، وَالنَّهَارُ مُضِيءٌ فَلاَ تُكَدِّرْهُ بِآثَامِكَ.

وَيَنْبَغِي أَنْ يَغْتَنِمَ الشُّيُوخَ وَيَسْتَفِيدَ مِنْهُمْ، وَلَيْسَ كُلُّ مَا فَاتَ يُدْرَكُ، كَمَا قَالَ أُسْتَاذُنَا شَيْخُ الإِسْلَامِ فِي «مَشْيَخَتِهِ»: كَمْ مِنْ شَيْخٍ كَبِيرٍ أَدْرَكْتُهُ وَمَا اسْتَخْبَرْتُهُ.

وَأَقُولُ عَلَى هٰذَا الْفَوْتِ مُنْشِئًا هٰذَا الْبَيْتَ:

لَهْفًا عَلَى فَوْتِ التَّلاقِي لَهْفَا ... مَا كُلُّ مَا فَاتَ وَيَفْنَى يُلْفَى

قَالَ عَلِيٌّ رَضِيَ اللّٰهُ عَنْهُ: إِذَا كُنْتَ فِي أَمْرٍ فَكُنْ فِيهِ، وَكَفَى بِالْإِعْرَاضِ عَنْ عِلْمِ اللَّهِ خِزْيًا وَخَسَارًا، وَاسْتَعِذْ بِاللَّهِ مِنْهُ لَيْلًا وَنَهَارًا.

وَلَا بُدَّ لِطَالِبِ الْعِلْمِ مِنْ تَحَمُّلِ الْمَشَقَّةِ وَالْمَذَلَّةِ فِي طَلَبِ الْعِلْمِ، وَالتَّمَلُّقُ مَذْمُومٌ إِلَّا فِي طَلَبِ الْعِلْمِ، فَإِنَّهُ لَا بُدَّ لَهُ مِنَ التَّمَلُّقِ لِلْأُسْتَاذِ وَالشَّرِيكِ وَغَيْرِهِمْ لِلاسْتِفَادَةِ مِنْهُمْ.

قِيلَ : الْعِلْمُ عِزٌّ لَا ذُلَّ فِيهِ، لَا يُدْرَكُ إِلَّا بِذُلٍّ لَا عِزَّ فِيهِ.

وَقَالَ الْقَائِلُ:

أَرَى لَكَ نَفْسًا تَشْتَهِي أَنْ تُعِزَّهَا ... فَلَسْتَ تَنَالُ الْعِزَّ حَتَّى تُذِلَّهَا

It is narrated that the Prophet ﷺ said: "Whoever is not pious in his pursuit of knowledge, Allah will afflict him with one of three things: an early death, life in a rural area, or servitude to rulers."

The more piety a student has, the more beneficial his knowledge becomes, the easier his learning becomes, and the greater his benefits multiply.

Complete piety entails refraining from overeating, excessive sleeping, and engaging in idle talk. A student should also avoid eating food sold in marketplaces, if possible. Such food is often associated with impurity, heedlessness, and a lack of Allah's remembrance. Moreover, the poor may gaze upon it without being able to afford it, which harms them and diminishes the food's blessing.

It is narrated that Shaykh al-Imām Muhammad ibn al-Faḍl refrained from eating market food during his studies. His father, who lived in the countryside, would prepare his meals and bring them to him on Fridays. One day, his father saw market bread in his son's house and became angry. When his son explained that the bread was brought by his companion, his father replied: "If you were cautious and pious, your companion would not dare to bring it."

Such was their piety, and thus they were blessed with success in knowledge and teaching. Their names endure to this day.

A pious jurist once advised a student of knowledge: "Beware of backbiting and avoid the company of excessive talkers." He said: "Those who speak excessively steal your time and waste your moments."

A student should also avoid the corrupt, the sinful, and the negligent while seeking the company of the righteous, for proximity influences behaviour. He should sit facing the qiblah, adhere to the Sunnah, and cherish the prayers of the pious

# فصل فِي الْوَرَعِ فِي حَالَةِ التَّعَلُّمِ

رَوَىٰ بَعْضُهُمْ حَدِيثًا فِي هَذَا الْبَابِ عَنْ رَسُولِ اللَّهِ ﷺ أَنَّهُ قَالَ: «مَنْ لَمْ يَتَوَرَّعْ فِي تَعَلُّمِهِ ابْتَلاهُ اللَّهُ تَعَالَىٰ بِأَحَدِ ثَلاثَةِ أَشْيَاءَ: إِمَّا أَنْ يُمِيتَهُ فِي شَبَابِهِ، أَوْ يُوقِعَهُ فِي الرَّسَاتِيقِ، أَوْ يَبْتَلِيهِ بِخِدْمَةِ السُّلْطَانِ»، فَكُلَّمَا كَانَ طَالِبُ الْعِلْمِ أَوْرَعَ كَانَ عِلْمُهُ أَنْفَعَ، وَالتَّعَلُّمُ لَهُ أَيْسَرُ وَفَوَائِدُهُ أَكْثَرُ.

وَمِنَ الْوَرَعِ [الْكَامِلِ] أَنْ يَتَحرَّزَ عَنِ الشِّبَعِ وَكَثْرَةِ النَّوْمِ، وَكَثْرَةِ الْكَلامِ فِيمَا لا يَنْفَعُ، وَأَنْ يَتَحَرَّزَ عَنْ أَكْلِ طَعَامِ السُّوقِ إِنْ أَمْكَنَ؛ لِأَنَّ طَعَامَ السُّوقِ أَقْرَبُ إِلَى النَّجَاسَةِ وَالْخَبَاثَةِ، وَأَبْعَدُ عَنْ ذِكْرِ اللَّهِ وَأَقْرَبُ إِلَى الْغَفْلَةِ؛ وَلِأَنَّ أَبْصَارَ الْفُقَرَاءِ تَقَعُ عَلَيْهِ وَلا يَقْدِرُونَ عَلَى الشِّرَاءِ مِنْهُ، فَيَتَأَذَّوْنَ بِذَلِكَ فَيُذْهَبُ بَرَكَتُهُ.

وَحُكِيَ أَنَّ الشَّيْخَ الْإِمَامَ الْجَلِيلَ مُحَمَّدَ بْنَ الْفَضْلِ كَانَ فِي حَالِ تَعَلُّمِهِ لا يَأْكُلُ مِن طَعَامِ السُّوقِ، وَكَانَ أَبُوهُ يَسْكُنُ فِي الرَّسَاتِيقِ، وَيُهَيِّئُ طَعَامَهُ وَيَدْخُلُ إِلَيْهِ يَوْمَ الْجُمُعَةِ، فَرَأَىٰ فِي بَيْتِ ابْنِهِ خُبْزَ السُّوقِ يَوْمًا فَلَمْ يُكَلِّمْهُ سَاخِطًا عَلَى ابْنِهِ فَاعْتَذَرَ ابْنُهُ، فَقَالَ: مَا اشْتَرَيْتُهُ أَنَا وَلَمْ أَرْضَ بِهِ؛ وَلَكِنْ أَحْضَرَهُ شَرِيكِي، فَقَالَ أَبُوهُ: لَوْ كُنْتَ تَحْتَاطُ وَتَتَوَرَّعُ عَنْ مِثْلِهِ، لَمْ يَجْرُؤْ شَرِيكُكَ عَلَىٰ ذَلِكَ.

وَهَكَذَا كَانُوا يَتَوَرَّعُونَ؛ فَلِذَلِكَ وُفِّقُوا لِلْعِلْمِ وَالنَّشْرِ حَتَّىٰ بَقِيَ اسْمُهُمْ إِلَىٰ يَوْمِ الْقِيَامَةِ.

while avoiding the curses of the wronged.

It is narrated that two men travelled abroad in search of knowledge. After several years, they returned to their homeland. One had become a jurist, while the other had not gained much understanding. Upon investigation, it was discovered that the one who succeeded always sat facing the qiblah and the city where they studied, while the other sat with his back to the qiblah and his face to than the city. The scholars concluded that the jurist attained his knowledge through the blessings of facing the qiblah – since it is Sunnah when sitting except in necessity – and benefiting from the prayers of the pious in the city; it is never empty of the people of good and the ascetics from the servants [of Allah]. It is clear that a slave [of Allah] prayed for him in the night.

### CONSISTENCY AND PRAYER

A student of knowledge must not neglect etiquettes and traditions, for neglecting etiquettes leads to missing Sunnahs, neglecting Sunnahs leads to missing obligations, and missing obligations ultimately leads to loss in the Hereafter.

It is said that a student should pray abundantly and perform his prayers with humility and attentiveness, as this greatly aids in acquiring and retaining knowledge.

Shaykh al-Imām al-Ḥajjāj Najm al-Dīn ʿUmar al-Nasafī composed the following lines:

*Be vigilant in adhering to commands and prohibitions,*
*Perform prayers consistently and attentively.*
*Strive in seeking the sciences of Shariah, and persevere,*
*With pure intentions, you will become a learned jurist [and] ḥāfiz.*[9]

(9) Translator: "The title Ḥāfiẓ al-Hadīth is attributed to a scholar who has comprehensively mastered the knowledge of one hundred thousand Hadiths along with

وَوَصَّىٰ فَقِيهٌ مِنْ زُهَّادِ الْفُقَهَاءِ طَالِبَ الْعِلْمِ: أَنْ يَتَحَرَّزَ عَنِ الْغِيبَةِ وَعَنْ مُجَالَسَةِ الْمِكْثَارِ.

وَقَالَ: مَنْ يُكْثِرُ الْكَلَامَ يَسْرِقُ عُمُرَكَ وَيُضَيِّعُ أَوْقَاتَكَ.

وَمِنَ الْوَرَعِ أَنْ يَجْتَنِبَ مِنْ أَهْلِ الْفَسَادِ وَالْمَعَاصِي وَالتَّعْطِيلِ، وَيُجَاوِرَ الصُّلَحَاءَ، فَإِنَّ الْمُجَاوَرَةَ مُؤَثِّرَةٌ، وَأَنْ يَجْلِسَ مُسْتَقْبِلَ الْقِبْلَةِ، وَأَنْ يَكُونَ مُسْتَنًّا بِسُنَّةِ النَّبِيِّ عَلَيْهِ الصَّلَاةُ وَالسَّلَامُ، وَيَغْتَنِمَ دَعْوَةَ أَهْلِ الْخَيْرِ، وَيَتَحَرَّزَ عَنْ دَعْوَةِ الْمَظْلُومِينَ.

وَحُكِيَ أَنَّ رَجُلَيْنِ خَرَجَا فِي طَلَبِ الْعِلْمِ لِلْغُرْبَةِ وَكَانَا شَرِيكَيْنِ فَرَجَعَا بَعْدَ سِنِينَ إِلَىٰ بَلَدِهِمَا وَقَدْ فَقِهَ أَحَدُهُمَا وَلَمْ يَفْقَهِ الْآخَرُ، فَتَأَمَّلَ فُقَهَاءُ الْبَلْدَةِ وَسَأَلُوا عَنْ حَالِهِمَا وَتَكْرَارِهِمَا وَجُلُوسِهِمَا، فَأُخْبِرُوا أَنَّ جُلُوسَ الَّذِي تَفَقَّهَ فِي حَالَ التَّكْرَارِ كَانَ مُسْتَقْبِلَ الْقِبْلَةِ، وَالْمِصْرَ [الَّذِي حَصَّلَ الْعِلْمَ فِيهِ]، وَالْآخَرُ كَانَ مُسْتَدْبِرَ الْقِبْلَةِ وَوَجْهُهُ إِلَىٰ غَيْرِ الْمِصْرِ. فَاتَّفَقَ الْفُقَهَاءُ وَالْعُلَمَاءُ أَنَّ الْفَقِيهَ فَقُهَ بِبَرَكَةِ اسْتِقْبَالِ الْقِبْلَةِ إِذْ هُوَ السُّنَّةُ فِي الْجُلُوسِ إِلَّا عِنْدَ الضَّرُورَةِ، وَبِبَرَكَةِ دُعَاءِ الْمُسْلِمِينَ فَإِنَّ الْمِصْرَ لَا يَخْلُو مِنَ الْعُبَّادِ وَأَهْلِ الْخَيْرِ وَالزُّهْدِ؛ فَالظَّاهِرُ أَنَّ عَابِدًا دَعَا لَهُ فِي اللَّيْلِ.

فَيَنْبَغِي لِطَالِبِ الْعِلْمِ أَلَّا يَتَهَاوَنَ بِالْآدَابِ وَالسُّنَنِ، فَإِنَّ مَنْ تَهَاوَنَ بِالْآدَابِ حُرِمَ السُّنَنَ، وَمَنْ تَهَاوَنَ بِالسُّنَنِ حُرِمَ الْفَرَائِضَ، وَمَنْ

*Ask your Lord to preserve your understanding,*
*For Allah is the best of protectors.*

He also said:

*Obey and strive; do not succumb to laziness,*
*For you will return to your Lord.*
*Do not sleep excessively, for the best among creation,*
*Slept but a little during the night.*

A student should carry a notebook at all times to review and record insights. It is said: "Whoever does not keep a notebook close will not retain wisdom in their heart." The notebook should always contain blank spaces for additional notes. An inkwell should also be kept nearby to record what is heard from scholars. And we already mentioned the Hadith of Hilāl ibn Yasār.

their texts (*matn*) and chains of transmission (*isnād*)." Muḥammad al-Khādimī, *Barīqah Maḥmūdiyyah fī Sharḥ Ṭarīqah Muḥammadiyyah wa Sharī'ah Nabawiyyah fī Sīrah Aḥmadiyyah*, al-Naw' al-Thānī: al-'Ulūm al-Munhī 'Anhā, p. 258, Maktabah al-Shāmilah.

تَهَاوَنَ بِالْفَرَائِضِ حُرِمَ الْآخِرَةَ.

وَبَعْضُهُمْ قَالُوا : هَذَا حَدِيثٌ عَنْ رَسُولِ اللَّهِ ﷺ.

وَيَنْبَغِي أَنْ يُكْثِرَ الصَّلَاةَ، وَيُصَلِّي صَلَاةَ الْخَاشِعِينَ، فَإِنَّ ذَلِكَ عَوْنٌ لَهُ عَلَى التَّحْصِيلِ وَالتَّعَلُّمِ.

وَأُنْشِدْتُ لِلشَّيْخِ الْإِمَامِ الْجَلِيلِ الزَّاهِدِ الْحَجَّاجِ نَجْمِ الدِّينِ عُمَرَ بْنِ مُحَمَّدٍ النَّسَفِيِّ:

كُنْ لِلْأَوَامِرِ وَالنَّوَاهِي حَافِظًا وَعَلَى الصَّلَاةِ مُوَاظِبًا وَمُحَافِظَا

وَاطْلُبْ عُلُومَ الشَّرْعِ وَاجْهَدْ وَاسْتَعِنْ بِالطَّيِّبَاتِ تَصِرْ فَقِيهًا حَافِظَا

وَاسْأَلْ إِلَهَكَ حِفْظَ حِفْظِكَ رَاغِبًا مِنْ فِضْلِهِ فَاللهُ خَيْرٌ حَافِظًا

وَقَالَ رَحْمَةُ اللهِ عَلَيْهِ:

أَطِيعُوا وَجِدُّوا وَلَا تَكْسَلُوا وَأَنْتُمْ إِلَى رَبِّكُمْ تُرْجَعُونَ

وَلَا تَهْجَعُوا فَخِيَارُ الْوَرَى قَلِيلًا مِنَ اللَّيْلِ مَا يَهْجَعُونَ

وَيَنْبَغِي أَنْ يَسْتَصْحِبَ دَفْتَرًا عَلَى كُلِّ حَالٍ لِيُطَالِعَهُ، وَقِيلَ: مَنْ لَمْ يَكُنِ الدَّفْتَرُ فِي كُمِّهِ لَمْ تَثْبُتِ الْحِكْمَةُ فِي قَلْبِهِ.

وَيَنْبَغِي أَنْ يَكُونَ فِي الدَّفْتَرِ بَيَاضٌ، وَيَسْتَصْحِبُ الْمِحْبَرَةَ لِيَكْتُبَ مَا يَسْمَعُ [مِنَ الْعُلَمَاءِ]. وَقَدْ ذَكَرْنَا حَدِيثَ هِلَالِ بْنِ يَسَارٍ.

The strongest causes of memory preservation are diligence, consistency, reducing food intake, praying at night, and reciting the Qur'an, especially by looking at it.

It is said: "Nothing enhances memory like recitation of the Qur'an by looking at its pages." The Prophet ﷺ said: "The best act of my Ummah is the recitation of the Qur'an by looking at it."[10]

Shaddād ibn Ḥakīm saw one of his brethren in a dream and asked: "What did you find to be most beneficial?" He replied: "Recitation of the Qur'an by looking at it."

When picking up a book, it is recommended to say:

*Bismillāh* (In the name of Allah), *Subḥānallāh* (Glory be to Allah), *Al-ḥamdulillāh* (Praise be to Allah), *Lā ilāha illā Allāh* (There is no deity but Allah), *Allāhu Akbar* (Allah is the Greatest), and *Lā ḥawla wa lā quwwata illā billāh al-'Aliyy al-'Aẓīm* (There is no power or strength except with Allah, the Most High, the Most Great), the amount of every letter written, and that will be written forever and ever in every moment of every time.

Additionally, it is praiseworthy to say after completing each act of writing:

"I believe in Allah, the One, the Unique, the Truth, alone without any partner, and I disbelieve in all else besides Him."

Abundant salutations upon the Prophet ﷺ are highly meritorious, for his remembrance is a mercy to the worlds.

Imām al-Shāfi'ī ؓ said:

*I complained to Wakī' about my poor memory,*
*So he guided me to abandon sins.*
*For knowledge is a favour from Allah,*
*And Allah's favour is not given to a sinner.*

(10) Translator: I did not find this Hadith.

## فَصلٌ: فِيمَا يُورِثُ الحِفْظَ، وَفِيمَا يُورِثُ النِّسيَانَ

وَأَقْوَىٰ أَسْبَابِ الحِفْظِ: الجِدُّ، وَالْمُوَاظَبَةُ، وَتَقْلِيلُ الْغِذَاءِ، وَصَلَاةُ اللَّيلِ، وَقِرَاءَةُ الْقُرْآنِ مِنْ أَسْبَابِ الحِفْظِ.

قِيلَ: لَيْسَ شَيْءٌ أَزْيَدَ لِلْحِفظِ مِنْ قِرَاءَةِ الْقُرْآنِ نَظَرًا، وَالْقِرَاءَةُ نَظَرًا أَفْضَلُ لِقَوْلِهِ عِلَيْهِ الصَّلَاةُ وَالسَّلَامُ: «أَفْضَلُ أَعْمَالِ أُمَّتِي قِرَاءَةُ الْقُرْآنِ نَظرًا»، وَرَأَىٰ شَدَّادُ بْنُ حَكِيمٍ بَعْضَ إِخْوَانِهِ فِي الْمَنَامِ، فَقَالَ لِأَخِيهِ: أَيُّ شَيْءٍ وَجَدْتَهُ أَنْفَعَ؟ قَالَ: قِرَاءَةُ الْقُرْآنِ نَظرًا.

وَيَقُولُ عِنْدَ رَفْعِ الْكِتَابِ: بِسْمِ اللهِ، وَسُبْحَانَ اللهِ، وَالْحَمْدُ لِلَّهِ، وَلَا إِلَهَ إِلَّا اللَّهُ، وَاللَّهُ أَكْبَرُ، وَلَا حَوْلَ وَلَا قُوَّةَ إِلَّا بِاللَّهِ الْعَلِيِّ الْعَظِيمِ الْعَزِيزِ الْعَلِيمِ، عَدَدَ كُلِّ حَرْفٍ كُتِبَ وَيَكْتُبُ أَبَدَ الْآبِدِينَ وَدَهْرَ الدَّاهِرِينَ.

وَيَقُولُ بَعْدَ كُلِّ مَكْتُوبَةٍ: آمَنْتُ بِاللهِ الْوَاحِدِ الْأَحَدِ الْحَقِّ، وَحْدَهُ لَا شَرِيكَ لَهُ، وَكَفَرْتُ بِمَا سِوَاهُ.

وَيُكْثِرُ الصَّلَاةَ عَلَى النَّبِيِّ عَلَيْهِ السَّلَامُ فَإِنَّ ذِكْرَهُ رَحْمَةٌ لِلْعَالَمِينَ.

[قَالَ الشَّافِعِيُّ رَحِمَهُ اللهُ]:

شَكَوْتُ إِلَى وَكِيعَ سُوءَ حِفْظِي ... فَأَرْشَدَنِي إِلَىٰ تَرْكِ الْمَعَاصِي
فَإِنَّ الحِفْظَ فَضْلٌ مِنْ إِلَهِ ... وَفَضْلُ اللهِ لَا يُعْطَى لِعَاصِي

### PRACTICES TO STRENGTHEN MEMORY

- Using *siwāk* (tooth-stick).
- Drinking honey.
- Eating frankincense mixed with sugar.
- Eating twenty-one red raisins on an empty stomach daily enhances memory and cures various ailments.
- Anything that reduces phlegm and bodily moisture increases memory, while anything that increases phlegm causes forgetfulness.

### CAUSES OF FORGETFULNESS

- Sins and excessive disobedience.
- Worries and preoccupations with worldly matters.
- Excessive involvement in worldly relationships and attachments.

We already mentioned that it is advised not to concern oneself with worldly matters excessively, for they harm without benefit. Worldly anxieties bring darkness to the heart, whereas concerns for the Hereafter bring light. The effect of these concerns manifests in prayer. Concern for worldly matters prevents good deeds. Concern for the Hereafter motivates towards good deeds. Engaging in prayer with humility and seeking knowledge removes worries and sadness.

As the esteemed Shaykh Naṣr ibn al-Ḥasan al-Marghīnānī expressed in his poem:

*Seek assistance from Naṣr ibn al-Ḥasan,*
*In every knowledge that is stored,*
*For this is what removes sorrow,*
*And all else is vain and unreliable.*

Similarly, the venerable Shaykh al-Imām al-Ajall Najm al-Dīn ʿUmar ibn Muhammad al-Nasafī wrote in a verse regarding his passion for learning:

وَالسِّوَاكُ وَشُرْبُ الْعَسَلِ وَأَكْلُ الْكُنْدُرِ مَعَ السُّكَّرِ وَأَكْلُ إِحْدَىٰ وَعِشْرِينَ زَبِيبَةً حَمْرَاءَ كُلَّ يَوْمٍ عَلَى الرِّيقِ يُورِثُ الْحِفْظَ، وَيَشْفِي مِنْ كَثِيرٍ مِنْ الْأَمْرَاضِ وَالْأَسْقَامِ، وَكُلُّ مَا يُقَلِّلُ الْبَلْغَمَ وَالرُّطُوبَاتِ يَزِيدُ فِي الْحِفْظِ، وَكُلُّ مَا يَزِيدُ فِي الْبَلْغَمِ يُورِثُ النِّسْيَانَ.

وَأَمَّا مَا يُورِثُ النِّسْيَانَ فَالْمَعَاصِي وَكَثْرَةُ الذُّنُوبِ وَالْهُمُومُ وَالْأَحْزَانُ فِي أُمُورِ الدُّنْيَا، وَكَثْرَةُ الاشْتِغَالِ وَالْعَلَائِقِ، وَقَدْ ذَكَرْنَا أَنَّهُ لَا يَنْبَغِي لِلْعَاقِلِ أَنْ يَهْتَمَّ لِأَمْرِ الدُّنْيَا لِأَنَّهُ يَضُرُّ وَلَا يَنْفَعُ، وَهُمُومُ الدُّنْيَا لَا تَخْلُو عَنِ الظُّلْمَةِ فِي الْقَلْبِ، وَهُمُومُ الْآخِرَةِ لَا تَخْلُو عَنِ النُّورِ فِي الْقَلْبِ، وَيَظْهَرُ أَثَرُهُ فِي الصَّلَاةِ، فَهَمُّ الدُّنْيَا يَمْنَعُهُ مِنَ الْخَيْرَاتِ، وَهَمُّ الْآخِرَةِ يَحْمِلُهُ عَلَيْهِ، وَالِاشْتِغَالُ بِالصَّلَاةِ عَلَى الْخُشُوعِ وَتَحْصِيلِ الْعِلْمِ يَنْفِي الْهَمَّ وَالْحَزَنَ، كَمَا قَالَ الشَّيْخُ نَصْرُ بْنُ الْحَسَنِ الْمَرْغِينَانِيُّ فِي قَصِيدَةٍ لَهُ:

اسْتَعِنْ نَصْرَ بْنَ الْحَسَنْ ... فِي كُلِّ عِلْمٍ يُخْتَزَنْ
ذَاكَ الَّذِي يَنْفِي الْحَزَنْ ... وَمَا سِوَاهُ بَاطِلٌ لَا يُؤْتَمَنْ

وَالشَّيْخُ الإِمَامُ الْأَجَلُّ نَجْمُ الدِّينِ عُمَرُ بْنُ مُحَمَّدٍ النَّسَفِيُّ، فِي أُمِّ وَلَدِهِ:

سَلَامٌ عَلَى مَنْ تَيَمَّتْنِي بِظَرْفِهَا ... وَلُمْعَةِ خَدِّهَا وَلَمْحَةِ طَرْفِهَا

*Peace upon her who captivated me with her elegance,*
*With the glow of her cheeks and the glimmer of her glance.*
*She bewitched and entranced me, a radiant beauty,*
*Confounding imaginations in her and her charm.*
*I said to her, Leave me be and excuse me,*
*For I am engrossed in pursuing knowledge and its unveiling.*
*I find in the quest for virtue, knowledge, and piety,*
*An enrichment greater than the allure of maidens and their fragrance.*

## CAUSES OF FORGETFULNESS IN KNOWLEDGE

Among the factors identified as contributing to forgetfulness of knowledge are:

- Eating fresh coriander.
- Consuming sour apples.
- Looking at the crucified.
- Reading epitaphs on graves.
- Passing between caravans of camels.
- Dropping live lice onto the ground.
- Undergoing cupping therapy on the nape of the neck.

All of these are said to impair memory.

سَبَتْنِي وَأَصْبَتْنِي فَتَاةٌ مَلِيحَةٌ تَحَيَّرَتِ الْأَوْهَامُ فِي كُنْهِ وَصْفِهَا
فَقُلْتُ: ذَرِينِي وَاعْذُرِينِي فَإِنَّنِي شُغِفْتُ بِتَحْصِيلِ الْعُلُومِ وَكَشْفِهَا
وَلِي فِي طِلَابِ الْفَضْلِ وَالْعِلْمِ وَالتُّقَى غِنًى عَنْ غِنَاءِ الْغَانِيَاتِ وَعَرْفِهَا

وَأَمَّا أَسْبَابِ نِسْيَانِ الْعِلْمِ:

فَأَكْلُ الْكُزْبَرَةِ الرَّطْبَةِ، وَالتُّفَاحِ الْحَامِضِ، وَالنَّظَرُ إِلَى الْمَصْلُوبِ، وَقِرَاءَةِ أَلْوَاحِ الْقُبُورِ، وَالْمُرُورُ بَيْنَ قِطَارِ الْجِمَالِ، وَإِلْقَاءُ الْقَمْلِ الْحَيِّ عَلَى الْأَرْضِ، وَالْحِجَامَةُ عَلَى نَقْرَةِ الْقَفَا، كُلُّهَا يُورِثُ النِّسْيَانَ.

## CAUSES OF SUSTENANCE, PREVENTION OF SUSTENANCE, AND INCREASE OR DECREASE IN LIFESPAN

It is essential for seekers of knowledge to possess strength and an understanding of what increases sustenance, lifespan, and health, so they may fully devote themselves to the pursuit of knowledge. Many books have been authored on this subject; here, I mention a few points concisely.

The Messenger of Allah ﷺ said: "Destiny can only be altered by supplication, and only righteousness increases one's lifespan. Indeed, a person may be deprived of sustenance due to a sin he commits." This Hadith establishes that committing sins leads to deprivation of sustenance. Particularly, lying causes poverty, as is corroborated by specific traditions. Similarly, sleeping during the morning (*subḥa*) prevents sustenance, and excessive sleep brings about poverty and a lack of knowledge.

One poet said:

*People find joy in fine clothes,*
*But gathering knowledge is in forsaking sleep.*

Another lamented:

*Is it not sorrowful that nights pass without benefit,*
*Yet they are still counted from one's life?*

And yet another urged:

*Rise in the night, O seeker, perhaps you may be guided.*
*How long will you sleep while life slips away?*

### ACTIONS THAT HINDER SUSTENANCE

Certain actions are believed to hinder sustenance, as derived from tradition and experience. These include:

- Sleeping unclothed.
- Urinating while unclothed.

## فصل: فِيمَا يَجْلِبُ الرِّزْقَ وَفِيمَا يَمْنَعُ وَمَا يَزِيدُ فِي الْعُمْرِ وَمَا يُنْقِصُ

ثُمَّ لَا بُدَّ لِطَالِبِ الْعِلْمِ مِنَ الْقُوةِ وَمَعْرِفَةِ مَا يَزِيدُ فِيهِ وَمَا يَزِيدُ فِي الْعُمْرِ وَالصَّحَةِ لِيَتَفَرَّغَ فِي طَلَبِ الْعِلْمِ، وَفِي كُلِّ ذَلِكَ صَنَّفُوا كُتُبًا، أَوْرَدْتُ بَعْضَهَا هُنَا عَلَىٰ سَبِيلِ الاخْتِصَارِ.

قَالَ رَسُولُ اللهِ ﷺ: «لا يُرَدُّ الْقَدَرُ إِلَّا بِالدُّعَاءِ، وَلَا يَزِيدُ فِي الْعُمْرِ إِلَّا الْبِرُّ، فَإِنَّ الرَّجُلَ لَيُحْرَمُ مِنَ الرِّزْقِ بِذَنْبٍ يُصِيبُهُ».

ثَبَتَ بِهَذَا الْحَدِيثِ أَنَّ ارْتِكَابَ الذَّنْبِ سَبَبُ حِرْمَانِ الرِّزْقِ خُصُوصًا الْكَذِبُ فَإِنَّهُ يُورِثُ الْفَقْرَ، وَقَدْ وَرَدَ فِيهِ حَدِيثٌ خَاصٌّ، وَكَذَا نَوْمُ الصُّبْحَةِ يَمْنَعُ الرِّزْقَ، وَكَثْرَةُ النَّوْمِ تُورِثُ الْفَقْرَ، وَفَقْرُ الْعِلْمِ أَيْضًا. قَالَ الْقَائِلُ:

سُرُورُ النَّاسِ فِي لُبْسِ اللِّبَاسِ ... وَجَمْعُ الْعِلْمِ فِي تَرْكِ النُّعَاسِ

وَقَالَ:

أَلَيْسَ مِنَ الْحُزْنِ أَنَّ لَيَالِيًا ... تَمُرُّ بلَا نَفْعٍ وَتُحْسَبُ مِنْ عُمُرِ

وَقَالَ أيضا:

قُمِ اللَّيْلَ يَا هٰذَا لَعَلَّكَ تَرْشُدُ ... إِلَىٰ كَمْ تَنَامُ اللَّيْلَ وَالْعُمْرُ يَنْفَدُ

وَالنَّوْمُ عُرْيَانًا، وَالْبَوْلُ عُرْيَنًا، وَالْأَكْلُ جُنُبًا، وَالْأَكْلُ مُتَّكِئاً عَلَىٰ

- Eating while in a state of impurity (*junub*).
- Eating while reclining on one's side.
- Neglecting spilled food (letting the food fall from the table).
- Burning the peels of onions and garlic.
- Sweeping the house at night with a cloth.
- Leaving garbage in the house.
- Walking ahead of elders or scholars.
- Calling one's parents by their names.
- Picking one's teeth with any wooden stick.
- Washing hands with soil or mud.
- Sitting on thresholds.
- Leaning on one side of a doorpost.
- Performing ablution in places of impurity.
- Stitching clothes while wearing them.
- Wiping the face with one's garment.
- Neglecting spider webs in the house.
- Being negligent in prayers.
- Rushing out of the mosque after the dawn prayer.
- Leaving for the marketplace too early and returning late.
- Buying leftover bread from the poor.
- Begging excessively.
- Cursing one's parents.
- Neglecting to cover utensils.
- Extinguishing lamps with one's breath.

All these are believed to bring about poverty, as supported by transmitted reports. Likewise writing with a defective pen, combing hair with a broken comb, neglecting to pray for one's parents, wearing a turban while seated, wearing trousers while standing, miserliness, excessive frugality, extravagance, laziness, and negligence in matters of importance. The Messenger of Allah ﷺ said: "Seek sustenance through charity", and early

جَنْبٍ، وَالتَّهَاوُنُ بِسُقُوطِ الْمَائِدَةِ، وَحَرْقُ قِشْرِ الْبَصَلِ وَالثُّومِ، وَكَنْسُ الْبَيْتِ فِي اللَّيْلِ بِالْمِنْدِيلِ، وَتَرْكُ الْقُمَامَةِ فِي الْبَيْتِ، وَالْمَشْيُ قُدَّامَ الْمَشَايِخِ، وَنِدَاءُ الْوَالِدَيْنِ بِاسْمِهِمَا، وَالْخِلَالُ بِكُلِّ خَشَبَةٍ، وَغَسْلُ الْيَدَيْنِ بِالطِّينِ وَالتُّرَابِ، وَالْجُلُوسُ عَلَى الْعَتَبَةِ، وَالِاتِّكَاءُ عَلَى أَحَدِ زَوْجَيِ الْبَابِ، وَالتَّوَضُّؤُ فِي الْمَبْرَزِ، وَخِيَاطَةُ الثَّوْبِ عَلَى بَدَنِهِ، وَتَجْفِيفُ الْوَجْهِ بِالثَّوْبِ، وَتَرْكُ بَيْتِ الْعَنْكَبُوتِ فِي الْبَيْتِ، وَالتَّهَاوُنُ فِي الصَّلَاةِ، وَإِسْرَاعُ الْخُرُوجِ مِنَ الْمَسْجِدِ بَعْدَ صَلَاةِ الْفَجْرِ، وَالِابْتِكَارُ بِالذَّهَابِ إِلَى السُّوقِ، وَالْإِبْطَاءُ فِي الرُّجُوعِ مِنْهُ، وَشِرَاءُ كِسْرَاتِ الْخُبْزِ مِنَ الْفُقَرَاءِ، وَالسُّؤَالُ، وَدُعَاءُ الشَّرِّ عَلَى الْوَالِدِ، وَتَرْكُ تَخْمِيرِ الْأَوَانِي، وَإِطْفَاءُ السِّرَاجِ بِالنَّفَسِ:

كُلُّ ذَلِكَ يُورِثُ الْفَقْرَ، عُرِفَ ذَلِكَ بِالْآثَارِ.

وَكَذَا الْكِتَابَةُ بِالْقَلَمِ الْمَعْقُودِ، وَالِامْتِشَاطُ بِالْمُشْطِ الْمُنْكَسِرِ، وَتَرْكُ الدُّعَاءِ لِلْوَالِدَيْنِ، وَالتَّعَمُّمُ قَاعِدًا، وَالتَّسَرْوُلُ قَائِمًا، وَالْبُخْلُ وَالتَّقْتِيرُ، وَالْإِسْرَافُ، وَالْكَسَلُ وَالتَّوَانِي وَالتَّهَاوُنُ فِي الْأُمُورِ.

وَقَالَ رَسُولُ اللَّهِ ﷺ:

«اسْتَنْزِلُوا الرِّزْقَ بِالصَّدَقَةِ»، وَالْبُكُورُ مُبَارَكٌ، يَزِيدُ فِي جَمِيعِ النِّعَمِ خُصُوصًا فِي الرِّزْقِ.

وَحُسْنُ الْخَطِّ مِنْ مَفَاتِيحِ الرِّزْقِ وَبَسْطُ الْوَجْهِ وَطِيبُ الْكَلَامِ يَزِيدُ فِي الْحِفْظِ وَالرِّزْقِ.

وَعَنِ الْحَسَنِ بْنِ عَلِيٍّ: «كَنْسُ الْفِنَاءِ وَغَسْلُ الْإِنَاءِ مَجْلَبَةٌ لِلْغِنَى».

rising is blessed, increasing all types of blessings, especially in sustenance. Good fortune is among the keys to sustenance, and a cheerful face and kind words increase memory and provision. Al-Ḥasan ibn ʿAlī ﵄ said: "Sweeping the courtyard and washing dishes bring about wealth."

### KEY PRACTICES TO ATTRACT SUSTENANCE

The most effective ways to attract sustenance include:

- Establishing prayer with proper reverence, mindfulness, and the correct performance of its physical components, obligations, and etiquettes.
- Performing the Ḍuḥā prayer, which is specifically praised.
- Reciting Sūrah al-Wāqiʿah at night before sleep.
- Reciting Sūrah al-Mulk, Sūrah al-Muzzammil, Sūrah al-Layl, and Sūrah al-Inshirāḥ.
- Attending the mosque before the call to prayer (*adhān*).
- Maintaining continuous purity (*wuḍūʾ*).
- Performing the Sunnah prayers of *fajr* and *witr* at home.
- Avoiding unnecessary worldly conversations after *witr*.
- Limiting one's association with women unless necessary.
- Avoiding frivolous talk.

It has been said: "Whoever busies himself with matters that do not concern him will lose matters that do." Buzrujumhḥr wisely remarked: "If you see a man speaking excessively, be certain of his foolishness." ʿAlī (may Allah ennoble his face) also said: "When intellect is perfected, speech becomes less."

The author ﵀ said:

*When a man's intellect is perfected, his words decrease;*
*Be assured of a fool's ignorance if he speaks excessively.*
*Speech is an adornment, silence is safety;*
*If you speak, do not overdo it.*
*Never have I regretted my silence,*
*But often have I regretted my words.*

وَأَقْوَى الْأَسْبَابِ الْجَاذِبَةِ لِلرِّزْقِ:

إِقَامَةُ الصَّلَاةِ بِالتَّعْظِيمِ وَالْخُشُوعِ،

وَتَعْدِيلُ الْأَرْكَانِ وَسَائِرِ وَاجِبَاتِهَا وَسُنَنِهَا وَآدَابِهَا،

وَصَلَاةُ الضُّحَى فِي ذَلِكَ مَعْرُوفَةٌ،

وَقِرَاءَةُ سُورَةِ الْوَاقِعَةِ خُصُوصًا فِي اللَّيْلِ وَقْتَ النَّوْمِ،

وَقِرَاءَةُ سُورَةِ الْمُلْكِ،

وَالْمُزَّمِّلُ،

﴿وَالَّيْلِ إِذَا يَغْشَى﴾،

﴿وَأَلَمْ نَشْرَحْ لَكَ صَدْرَكَ﴾،

وَحُضُورُ الْمَسْجِدِ قَبْلَ الْأَذَانِ،

وَالْمُدَاوَمَةُ عَلَى الطَّهَارَةِ،

وَأَدَاءُ سُنَّةِ الْفَجْرِ وَالْوِتْرِ فِي الْبَيْتِ،

وَأَلَّا يَتَكَلَّمَ بِكَلَامِ الدُّنْيَا بَعْدَ الْوِتْرِ وَلَا يُكْثِرَ مُجَالَسَةَ النِّسَاءِ إِلَّا عِنْدَ الْحَاجَةِ، وَأَلَّا يَتَكَلَّمَ بِكَلَامِ لَغْوٍ.

وَقِيلَ: مَنِ اشْتَغَلَ بِمَا لَا يَعْنِيهِ فَاتَهُ مَا يَعْنِيهِ. قَالَ بُزُرْجُمْهُر: إِذَا رَأَيْتَ الرَّجُلَ يُكْثِرُ الْكَلَامَ فَاسْتَيْقِنْ بِجُنُونِهِ. وَقَالَ عَلِيٌّ: «إِذَا تَمَّ الْعَقْلُ نَقَصَ الْكَلَامُ».

قَالَ الْمُصَنِّفُ رَحِمَهُ اللهُ: وَاتَّفَقَ لِي فِي هَذَا الْمَعْنَى شِعْرًا:

As for what increases sustenance:

- To say every day after the break of dawn (*inshiqāq al-fajr*) until the time of prayer (*ṣalāh*): *Subḥāna Allāhi al-ʿAẓīmi wa biḥamdihi, Subḥāna Allāhi al-ʿAẓīmi wa biḥamdihi, wa astaghfiru Allāha al-ʿAẓīma wa atūbu ilayhi* (Glory be to Allah the Magnificent and with His Praise, I seek Allah's forgiveness, the Magnificent, and I repent to Him) one hundred times.
- To say:*Lā ilāha illā Allāhu al-Maliku al-Ḥaqqu al-Mubīn* (There is no deity but Allah, the King, the Absolute Truth, the Clear One) every morning and evening one hundred times.
- To say after the morning (*fajr*) prayer (*ṣalāh*) every day: *Al-ḥamdulillāh, wa subḥāna Allāh, wa lā ilāha illā Allāh, wa Allāhu akbar* (All praise is due to Allah, glory be to Allah, there is no deity but Allah, and Allah is the Greatest) thirty-three times, and after the evening (*maghrib*) prayer as well.
- To seek forgiveness from Allah (*astaghfiru Allāh taʿālā*) seventy times after the morning (*fajr*) prayer.
- To frequently say: *Lā ḥawla wa lā quwwata illā billāhi al-ʿAliyyi al-ʿAẓīm* (There is no power or might except with Allah, the Most High, the Magnificent).
- To send blessings upon the Prophet ﷺ.
- To say on Fridays (*yawm al-jumuʿah*) seventy times: *Allāhumma aghninī biḥalālika ʿan ḥarāmika wa akfinī bi-faḍlika ʿamman siwāka* (O Allah, suffice me with Your lawful sustenance instead of the forbidden, and enrich me with Your grace from needing others besides You).

And one should recite this praise (*thanāʾ*) every day and night:

*Anta Allāhu al-ʿAzīzu al-Ḥakīm, Anta Allāhu al-Maliku*

إِذَا تَمَّ عَقْلُ الْمَرْءِ قَلَّ كَلَامُهُ     وَأَيْقِنْ بِحُمْقِ الْمَرْءِ إِنْ كَانَ مُكْثِرَا
النُّطْقُ زَيْنٌ وَالسُّكُوتُ سَلَامَةٌ     فَإِذَا نَطَقْتَ فَلَا تَكُونَ مِكْثَارَا
مَا نَدِمْتُ عَلَى سُكُوتٍ مَرَّةً     وَلَقَدْ نَدِمْتُ عَلَى الْكَلَامِ مِرَارًا

وَأَمَّا مَا يَزِيدُ فِي الرِّزْقِ:

- أَنْ يَقُولَ كُلَّ يَوْمٍ بَعْدَ انْشِقَاقِ الْفَجْرِ إِلَىٰ وَقْتِ الصَّلَاةِ: سُبْحَانَ اللَّهِ الْعَظِيمِ وَبِحَمْدِهِ، سُبْحَانَ اللَّهِ الْعَظِيمِ وَبِحَمْدِهِ، وَأَسْتَغْفِرُ اللهَ الْعَظِيمَ وَأَتُوبُ إِلَيْهِ، مِائَةَ مَرَّةٍ،

- وَأَنْ يَقُولَ: «لَا إِلَهَ إِلَّا اللَّهُ الْمَلِكُ الْحَقُّ الْمُبِينُ»، كُلَّ يَوْمٍ صَبَاحًا وَمَسَاءً مِائَةَ مَرَّةٍ.

- وَأَنْ يَقُولَ بَعْدَ صَلَاةِ الْفَجْرِ كُلَّ يَوْمٍ: «الْحَمْدُ للهِ، وَسُبْحَانَ اللَّهِ، وَلَا إِلَهَ إِلَّا اللَّهُ وَاللَّهُ أَكْبَرُ، ثَلَاثًا وَثَلَاثِينَ مَرَّةً، وَبَعْدَ صَلَاةِ الْمَغْرِبِ أَيْضًا.

- وَيَسْتَغْفِرُ اللهَ تَعَالَىٰ سَبْعِينَ مَرَّةً بَعْدَ صَلَاةِ الْفَجْرِ،

- وَيُكْثِرُ مِنْ قَوْلِ: «لَا حَوْلَ وَلَا قُوَّةَ إِلَّا بِاللهِ الْعَلِيِّ الْعَظِيمِ»، وَالصَّلَاةِ عَلَى النَّبِيِّ ﷺ.

وَيَقُولُ يَوْمَ الْجُمُعَةِ سَبْعِينَ مَرَّةً: «اللَّهُمَّ أَغْنِنِي بِحَلَالِكَ عَنْ حَرَامِكَ وَاكْفِنِي بِفَضْلِكَ عَمَّنْ سِوَاكَ».

- وَيَقُولُ هذا الثَّنَاءَ كُلَّ يَوْمٍ وَلَيْلَةٍ: «أَنْتَ اللهُ الْعَزِيزُ الْحَكِيمُ، أَنْتَ اللَّهُ الْمَلِكُ الْقُدُّوسُ، أَنْتَ اللَّهُ الْحَكِيمُ الْكَرِيمُ، أَنْتَ اللهُ خَالِقُ الْخَيْرِ وَالشَّرِّ، أَنْتَ اللهُ خَالِقُ الْجَنَّةِ وَالنَّارِ، أَنْتَ اللهُ عَالِمُ الْغَيْبِ

*al-Quddūs, Anta Allāhu al-Ḥakīmu al-Karīm, Anta Allāhu Khāliqu al-Khayri wa al-Sharri, Anta Allāhu Khāliqu al-Jannati wa al-Nār, Anta Allāhu ʿĀlimu al-Ghaybi wa al-Shahādah, Anta Allāhu ʿĀlimu al-Sirri wa Akhfā, Anta Allāhu al-Kabīru al-Mutaʿāl, Anta Allāhu Khāliqu Kulli Shayʾin, wa ilayhi yaʿūdu kullu shayʾ, Anta Allāhu Dayyānu Yawmi al-Dīn, Lam tazal wa lā tazāl, Anta Allāhu lā ilāha illā Anta al-Aḥad,*

(quoting from Sūrah al-Ikhlāṣ):

*Allāhu al-Ṣamad, Lam yalid wa lam yūlad, wa lam yakun lahu kufuwan aḥad.*
*Anta Allāhu lā ilāha illā Anta al-Raḥmānu al-Raḥīm, Anta Allāhu lā ilāha illā Anta,*

(quoting from Sūrah al-Hashr):

*Al-Malik al-Quddūs al-Salām al-Muʾmin al-Muhaymin al-ʿAzīz al-Jabbār al-Mutakabbir,*
*Lā ilāha illā Anta,*

(quoting from Sūrah al-Hashr):

*Al-Khāliqu al-Bāriʾu al-Muṣawwiru, Lahu al-Asmāʾ al-Ḥusnā, Yusabbiḥu lahu mā fī al-samāwāti wa al-arḍ wa huwa al-ʿAzīzu al-Ḥakīm.*

What Increases One's Lifespan (*ʿUmr*):

- *Al-birr* (righteousness).
- *Tark al-adhā* (abandoning harm).
- *Tawqīr al-shuyūkh* (respecting the elders).
- *Ṣilat al-rahim* (maintaining family ties).

One should also recite morning and evening, every day, three times:

*Subḥāna Allāh milʾa al-mīzān, wa muntahā al-ʿilm, wa mablagh al-riḍā, wa zinata al-ʿarsh.*
*Wa al-ḥamdulillāh milʾa al-mīzān, wa muntahā al-ʿilm, wa*

وَالشَّهَادَةِ، أَنْتَ اللهُ عَالِمُ السِّرِ وَأَخفَىٰ، أَنْتَ اللهُ الْكَبِيرُ الْمُتَعَالِ، أَنْتَ اللَّهُ خَالِقُ كُلِّ شَيْءٍ، وَإِلَيْهِ يَعُودُ كُلُّ شَيْءٍ، أَنْتَ اللهُ دَيَّانُ يَوْمِ الدِّينِ، لَمْ تَزَلْ وَلَا تَزَالُ، أَنْتَ اللَّهُ لَا إِلَهَ إِلَّا أَنْتَ الْأَحَدُ ﴿اللهُ الصَّمَدُ لَمْ يَلِدْ وَلَمْ يُولَدْ وَلَمْ يَكُن لَّهُ كُفُوًا أَحَدٌ﴾ [الإخلاص]. أَنْتَ اللهُ لَا إِلَهَ إِلَّا أَنْتَ الرَّحْمَنُ الرَّحِيمُ، أَنْتَ اللهُ لَا إِلَهَ إِلَّا أَنْتَ، ﴿الْمَلِكُ الْقُدُّوسُ السَّلَامُ الْمُؤْمِنُ الْمُهَيْمِنُ الْعَزِيزُ الْجَبَّارُ الْمُتَكَبِّرُ﴾ [الحشر ٢٣]، لَا إِلَهَ إِلَّا أَنْتَ ﴿الْخَالِقُ الْبَارِئُ الْمُصَوِّرُ لَهُ الْأَسْمَاءُ الْحُسْنَى يُسَبِّحُ لَهُ مَا فِي السَّمَوَاتِ وَالْأَرْضِ وَهُوَ الْعَزِيزُ الْحَكِيمُ﴾ [الحشر].

وَأَمَّا مَا يَزِيدُ فِي الْعُمْرِ: الْبِرُّ، وَتَرْكُ الْأَذَىٰ، وَتَوْقِيرُ الشُّيُوخِ، وَصِلَةُ الرَّحِمِ.

- وَأَنْ يَقُولَ حِينَ يُصْبِحُ وَيُمْسِي كُلَّ يَوْمٍ ثَلَاثَ مَرَّاتٍ: «سُبْحَانَ اللَّهِ مِلْءَ الْمِيزَانِ، وَمُنْتَهَى الْعِلْمِ، وَمَبْلَغَ الرِّضَا، وَزِنَةَ الْعَرْشِ.

- وَالْحَمْدُ للهِ مِلْءَ الْمِيزَانِ، وَمُنْتَهَى الْعِلْمِ، وَمَبْلَغَ الرِّضَا، وَزِنَةَ الْعَرْشِ.

- وَاللهُ أَكْبَرُ، مِلْءَ الْمِيزَانِ، وَمُنْتَهَى الْعِلْمِ، وَمَبْلَغَ الرِّضَا، وَزِنَةَ الْعَرْشِ.

- وَأَنْ يَتَحَرَّزَ عَنْ قَطْعِ الْأَشْجَارِ الرَّطِبَةِ إِلَّا عِنْدَ الضَّرُورَةِ، وَإِسْبَاغُ الْوُضُوءِ، وَالصَّلَاةُ بِالتَّعْظِيمِ، وَقِرَاءَةُ الْقُرْآنِ، وَالْقِرَانُ بَيْنَ الْحَجِّ

*mablagh al-riḍā, wa zinata al-'arsh. Wa Allāhu akbar mil'a al-mīzān, wa muntahā al-'ilm, wa mablagh al-riḍā, wa zinata al-'arsh.*

Additional Practices:

*Avoid cutting live trees (ashjār al-raṭibah) except out of necessity.*
*Perform ablution (isbagh al-wuḍū') thoroughly.*
*Pray (ṣalāh) with reverence (ta'ẓīm) and humility.*
*Recite the Qur'an (qirā'ah al-Qur'ān).*
*Combine Hajj and 'Umrah (qirān bayna al-hajj wa al-'umrah).*
*Maintain health (ḥifẓ al-ṣiḥḥah).*

One should also learn some knowledge of medicine (*ṭibb*) and benefit from the Prophetic traditions in medicine (*aḥādīth al-ṭibb*) compiled by Imām Abū al-'Abbās al-Mustaghfirī in his famous book *Ṭibb al-Nabī* ﷺ, which is readily available for those who seek it.

All praise is due to Allah for completion, and may Allah send blessings upon our master Muhammad, the best of the noble messengers, and upon his family and his companions, the distinguished leaders, throughout the passage of ages and succession of days. *Āmīn.*

وَالْعُمْرَةِ، وَحِفْظُ الصِّحَةِ، وَلَا بُدَّ مِنْ أَنْ يَتَعَلَّمَ شَيْئًا مِنَ الطِّبِّ، وَيَتَبَرَّكَ بِالْآثَارِ الْوَارِدَةِ فِي الطِّبِّ الَّتِي جَمَعَهَا الْإِمَامُ أَبُو الْعَبَّاسِ الْمُسْتَغْفِرِيّ فِي كِتَابِهِ الْمُسَمَّىٰ بـ «بِطِبِّ النَّبِيِّ عَلَيْهِ السَّلَامُ»، يَجِدُهُ مَنْ يَطْلُبُهُ، فَهُوَ كِتَابٌ مَشْهُورٌ.

وَالْحَمْدُ للهِ عَلَى التَّمَامِ، وَصَلَّى اللهُ عَلَىٰ سَيِّدِنَا مُحَمَّدٍ أَفْضَلِ الرُّسُلِ الْكِرَامِ، وَآلِهِ وَصَحْبِهِ الْأَئِمَّةِ الْأَعْلَامِ، عَلَىٰ مَمَرِّ الدُّهُورِ وَتَعَاقُبِ الْأَيَّامِ، آمِين.

www.ingramcontent.com/pod-product-compliance
Lightning Source LLC
Chambersburg PA
CBHW030843090426
42737CB00009B/1094
*9781966329008*